CINCINNATI FOOD

A HISTORY OF QUEEN CITY CUISINE

POLLY CAMPBELL

AMERICAN PALATE

Published by American Palate
A Division of The History Press
Charleston, SC
www.historypress.com

A charcuterie plate from Panino, a now-closed restaurant in Over-the-Rhine.
Photograph by the author.

First published 2020

Manufactured in the United States

ISBN 9781467141529

Library of Congress Control Number: 2020934425

CONTENTS

Acknowledgements 5
Introduction 7

1. Arnold's Bar and Grill: Having a Drink with History 9
2. Porkopolis and the *Pigasus* Episode 13
3. Catawba Wine and the Queen City of the West 23
4. The Germans Arrive in Over-the-Rhine 29
5. The Meats We Eat 37
6. The People's Market: Findlay Market 49
7. From Farm to Table 61
8. Ice Cream and the Stubborn Graeters 74
9. Kaffee und Kuchen and the Neighborhood Bakery 83
10. Beer: Twice the National Average 90
11. Playing Under the Bright Lights of Vine Street 104
12. Cincinnati's Three Way: Our Chili 116
13. The Five-Star City: Fine Dining 127
14. Sacred Heart, Ravioli and Pizza: The Cincinnati Italians 143
15. Made in Cincinnati 153

About the Author 160

ACKNOWLEDGEMENTS

I have to thank my keen-eyed husband, Neil Sharrow, for proofreading and for eating all over Cincinnati with me for the last twenty-five years. And thanks to Raúl Arias and to all of the wonderful photographers at the *Cincinnati Enquirer*, whose photographs I was lucky to be able to include in this book.

INTRODUCTION

Cincinnati surprises people. People who haven't been here often assume it's an uninteresting Midwestern city, bland and conservative, with a weird name. But Cincinnati has depths. It has plenty of quirks. And mostly, it has history. The Ohio River, which moves in a graceful crescent, separating downtown Cincinnati from its historic Northern Kentucky neighbors, tells a story of settlement and western expansion. The blocks of brick rowhouses with ornate cornices and German inscriptions in a neighborhood called Over-the-Rhine tell of German immigration, while imposing public buildings, like City Hall and Music Hall, tell of the prosperity that came from meatpacking and soap-making and of the civic-mindedness of the city's citizens. The food that is unique in Cincinnati—its sausages and chili—has history, too.

Cincinnati is not my hometown—I moved here in the 1980s—but I've been discovering the food history of my new city since I was lucky enough to be hired by the *Cincinnati Enquirer* as a restaurant and food writer in 1996. At that time, Cincinnati was pretty conservative, politically and culturally, and it was somewhat complacent (if you can characterize an entire city that way). Of course, there were always innovative people who made waves and changes, both good and bad. But things had been settled for a long time. Cincinnati peaked early, as it was the first real city of the West. It dazzled in the first part of the nineteenth century, but after the Civil War, other cities took over, attracted immigrants and made forward-looking decisions. Of course, changes happened here along with the rest of the country through the twentieth century (like the building of interstates, industrialization, suburban growth, racial reckonings, civic tragedies, et cetera). Our diet changed along with everyone else's, too, moving toward convenience foods and chain restaurants, national brands and food imported from farther and farther away.

But during this long period of slow change, Cincinnati hung onto certain things to eat that were unique to this city. Regional foods were dying everywhere, but our population held onto certain foods and brands that were eaten here as a matter of habit—unremarked on and not marketed to the rest of the world. We went to neighborhood butchers and bakers, ate our German-inspired meats and drank our local beer.

Throughout my time at the *Enquirer*, so much has happened in food and dining in Cincinnati, just as it has across the country. People started eating out more and restaurants became better, not just in fine dining, but at all levels of price and formality. An enthusiasm for local food grew. Television got people interested in regional differences and unusual places to eat. The food scene here got interesting and more varied.

Cincinnati was obviously not alone in this steady growth of food innovation, nor was it a leader—the city was doing it its own way. I noticed that many of the best ideas were inspired by the city's history. Old institutions, like butchers, ice cream shops and the historic public market, had been around forever, stubbornly doing their thing for years, and they began to flourish under this new attention. And what seemed new—farmers' markets, beer, cocktails—were inspired by history. In a place with as much history as Cincinnati, that's a lot of inspiration.

Today, eateries in Cincinnati can be as modern and bland as chain restaurants that could be anywhere, as contemporary as gastronomic food tasting menus, as innovative as ranching fish for caviar (see chapter 11), as traditional as sauerbraten in a diner or as mixed up and fun as eating gourmet hot dogs made by a traditional butcher in a restaurant on a street that was once the scene of nineteenth-century revelry.

This book tells the story of Cincinnati's traditional beloved things and food that have lasted through both change and complacency. It also tells the stories of people who wanted to do something new and take their cue from history. I don't claim to tell the entire history of Cincinnati food in this book or take a deep dive into each topic; I only concentrated on the foods and the places that are still with us or that inspired the food we eat today. I'm writing this introduction in the middle of the 2020 coronavirus crisis, and the future of our food history is not at all clear. Surely, though, the special flavor of Cincinnati will endure.

1

ARNOLD'S BAR AND GRILL

Having a Drink with History

Let's start this look at Cincinnati's food history in a place where anyone can sit with a glass of beer and a pretzel and feel transported to a couple of different points in our history. At Arnold's Bar and Grill on Eighth Street in downtown Cincinnati, the oldest eating and drinking establishment in town, it's easy to imagine its original era and the eras in which its original history was brought back to life. Arnold's is one of Cincinnati's most beloved spots, and there is history in every corner.

For many people, the television show *WKRP in Cincinnati* is the first thing to come to mind on hearing the city's name (although, since it went off the air more than thirty years ago, fewer people recognize it today than they have in the past). Twenty-nine years later, Cincinnati was, once again, the setting for a television show called *Harry's Law*. The show lasted for two seasons, between 2011 and 2012. Kathy Bates played a lawyer whose office was in a shoe store. For the second season, the producers wanted to work more of Cincinnati into the show and started having Bates's character spend more time at a bar called Arnold's. The show's bar was modeled after the real Arnold's in Cincinnati. The set designers reproduced Arnold's special look and feeling, with its historic features, worn linoleum and old prints, photographs and beer advertisements. It's the sort of bar that doesn't exist much anymore, but almost everyone recognizes it as a gem.

I wrote about Arnold's in 2011, when the bar turned 150 years old. Ronda Breeden owned it then. We walked up the stairs and noticed the deep grooves in the center of each wooden step. They reminded her of all who came before. "I think about everyone who's owned this place and the kind of heart they had to have," she said. "They made it through some hard times." The bar has had hard times from its beginning. Simon Arnold opened it as a saloon in 1861, the same year the Civil War started. (If you're imagining historic eras, think of celebrating the end of that national nightmare at this Cincinnati bar with a beer.) The city was mostly confined to the basin between the Ohio River and the Vine Street Hill, and Germans had begun swelling the population. There is no doubt that many of Arnold's patrons were German, standing (never sitting) at the bar, one foot on the brass rail.

Simon owned the bar for a long time—until about 1900, when his son Hugo took it over. Hugo added the building next door, which allowed for a separate entrance and room for women. Hugo, his wife and their six children lived on the second and third floors of the bar's building. One of those children, Elmer Arnold, took over the bar in the 1920s, during Prohibition. Since he couldn't sell alcohol—at least not openly—he was the first owner of Arnold's to serve food. He was most likely selling homemade gin. It was probably mixed in the bathtub because it was easy to pull the plug in case there was a raid. That claw-foot bathtub is still in one of the upstairs rooms, and it is the icon of Arnold's.

In 1959, brothers Jim Christakos and George Christos (George had simplified his last name) took over the bar and established a sort of luncheonette there. Visitors today can see a mural of waitresses in uniform out in the courtyard. At that time, the luncheonette served at least one Greek dish: a simple dish of spaghetti tossed with olive oil, garlic sauce, bacon and Romano that they called Greek spaghetti. The spaghetti is still on the menu because when Jim Tarbell bought the business from Alex Chaldekas in 1976, he preserved the dish, along with the building's antique spirit.

Tarbell was a young guy with a big red beard and a hippy-ish head of hair. He had grown up in Hyde Park and had run a church youth club that brought in the Grateful Dead early in the band's career. He then owned The Ludlow Garage in Clifton, where other legendary bands played (the Allman Brothers Band even recorded a live album there). He lived in downtown Cincinnati with friends on Court Street. They were musicians, artists and craftspeople who called themselves the Court Street Irregulars, and they had a potluck club that needed a permanent home. He stopped in at Arnold's one day and found a discouraged Chaldekas who was thinking of selling. Downtown Cincinnati was not doing well, and his customers had moved to the suburbs. Tarbell raised enough money to buy the business and turned it into a bar and restaurant that reflected its 1970s counter-culture milieu.

Jim Tarbell, the owner of Arnold's from 1976 to 1998, surveying the courtyard in 1978. *Courtesy of the* Cincinnati Enquirer *and Dick Swaim.*

Tarbell didn't have the money for big renovations, but he wouldn't have changed much anyway. He loved antiques, old things and the history of his city. He and his friends dragged an old bar in to replace what had been there originally. They also covered the walls with donated and scrounged art and began offering live music by musicians who played jug band music, bluegrass or blues, including Cincinnati blues legend Pigmeat Jarrett. One day, Tarbell used a sledgehammer to smash through the bar's wall into what is now the courtyard, and he put tables out there.

Tarbell's wife, Brenda, created Arnold's first menu. The couple got the old Greek spaghetti recipe from Chaldekas and put it on the menu, where it's been ever since, along with a deluxe version that has tomatoes, green peppers, mushrooms and olives. Two women who had been running a catering business, Antonia Davena and Mary McMahon, were the next people in charge of Arnold's kitchen. Davena, who was from a big Italian family, made her own pasta. "They'd be upstairs at a big table, rolling out pasta in the morning," remembered Tarbell. "It was poetry." Davena's dish of tomato sauce and meatballs has never lost its spot on the menu. The food at Arnold's has always been hearty and not too expensive; it kept up with the times, but it was never trendy. Tarbell championed good beer, serving Guinness when it first became available in America. He was also the first to put Christian Moerlein, a revived local brand (you'll see the name again in chapter 10), on tap. The first Moerlein kegs to arrive at Arnold's were delivered in a horse-drawn cart.

Arnold's has been improvisatory, a little zany and a lot of fun ever since Tarbell's time. Parked in front of the building, with its old green awning, is a smaller version of the famous bathtub; it's hooked up with wheels and a lawnmower engine so that it can participate in parades, particularly the annual spring Bockfest Parade that celebrates bock beer and always begins at Arnold's. "I never had a bad day at Arnold's," Tarbell told me. He later lost all of his hair and went on to run for city council. He became a well-known figure in the city, recognized for his love of his hometown and its history, and he is often called Mr. Cincinnati. There's even a big mural of him dressed as Peanut Jim, an old-time African American hawker of peanuts at Reds games, on the side of a building at Central Parkway and Vine. He eventually sold the restaurant to Ronda Breeden in 1999.

Breeden ran into hard times after there were riots downtown in 2001, but she persevered and eventually managed to buy the building. In 2020, she passed the restaurant on to her son Chris Breeden, who had been helping her run it. Chris took on an icon. It's a tricky place to own; the old regulars would be aghast by any changes, but all old buildings and menus need refurbishing and fixing from time to time. The building is a constant reminder of Cincinnati's past and of how history can be revived to lend depth and soul to modern uses. Arnold's is a great first stop for anyone new to Cincinnati to get to know the city and imagine its history.

2
PORKOPOLIS AND THE *PIGASUS* EPISODE

When it comes to repurposing the past and mining it for modern use, there's no better example than the *Pigasus* episode, when Cincinnati learned to shine up something that seemed old and disreputable. Cincinnati reached its bicentennial in 1988. Two hundred years before, a few flatboats had pulled up on the northern side of the Ohio River, opposite of the Licking River, and small parties began making homes in the wilderness. This community, which they called Losantiville, eventually grew into the city that exists today. Cincinnati went all-out to celebrate the two hundred years since that first landing.

A beautiful new park called Bicentennial Commons was built on the riverfront; the park contains historical markers, a statue of the city's namesake, Cincinnatus, and other reminders of Ohio River history. The Bicentennial Commission held a contest for an installation at the entrance to the park. The winning design was submitted by Minneapolis artist Andrew Leicester. He had done his research and incorporated many elements of Cincinnati history into his grand sculpture, which featured canals, the seven hills and the stacks of steamboats. Perched on top of the smokestacks were four winged pigs standing on their hind legs, a nod to the pork packing industry that gave the city its start. Though the sculpture had no name, it was dubbed *Pigasus* after Leicester waxed eloquent in an interview about how his pigs represented "the angelic spirits of all the pigs that were slaughtered and were building blocks of Cincinnati's prosperity."

Flying pigs top the steamboat stacks on a bicentennial sculpture in downtown's Bicentennial Commons. *Courtesy of Raúl Arias.*

As historically correct and innocuous as this sounds, some Cincinnatians were really, really not happy with *Pigasus*. Letters to the editor in the *Enquirer* were indignant. "Pigs are not appropriate to Sawyer Point or to our image, much less a progressive image to live with in the next century," declared one writer. "I have raised hogs, I have castrated hogs and I have slaughtered hogs, and that is all part of reality. But I do not go around with a red-tinted flying pigs brooch on my power suit lapel," scolded another. Mayor Charles Luken chimed in, saying, "I think we risk a lot of embarrassment from people who come here from outside the area....I think most people will wonder 'Why did Cincinnati put Porky Pig on a piece of sculpture?'" Councilman Steve Chabot said he "wasn't pro-pig or anti-pig," but he thought city council should vote on whether to include them in the sculpture.

It was what many would say was a typical Cincinnati response, a worry about how the city might be seen by others, an unacknowledged inferiority complex and a lack of a sense of humor. Well, that attitude did not prevail. A trip to Bicentennial Commons now shows that the "pro-pig" faction won this one. The pigs are still there, proudly pointing their snouts to the sky. In fact, pigs are everywhere. In 2000, the city held the Big Pig Gig, one of those city-wide street art projects that had local artists decorating fiberglass pig statues. There's been a restaurant called Porkopolis in the Mount Adams neighborhood, not to mention various dishes of the same name in other restaurants. The city's annual marathon is called the Flying Pig, or just the Pig, and plenty of people run it in pink snouts.

But the anti-piggers had a point. Pink pigs with cute little wings have, in a way, whitewashed what was a smelly and grimy business, one that Cincinnati has taken plenty of insults for in the past. Andrew Leicester had not driven down Central Parkway when the stockyards and slaughterhouses were in production and at full stink—then again, neither have most Cincinnatians. "Porkopolis" was never meant as a compliment, but Americans aren't supposed to be embarrassed by humble origins, especially if they can dress them up a little. The transformation of slaughtered hogs to cute pink pigs is surely the best re-branding Cincinnati has ever done. Unlike other committee-created nicknames like "Blue Chip City," "Porkopolis" is real. It's based on the city's true history.

Meat brought Cincinnati its first prosperity. When the United States as a nation was new and growing, Cincinnati-packed meat fed the earliest settlers of Ohio, the growing eastern cities and the hungry nation that was busy expanding westward after the Revolutionary War. In 1787, the new U.S. Congress passed the Northwest Ordinance, laying out how the nation was to grow. It was not to expand by a sort of colony system in which new lands served merely as resources for the existing states, nor was it to grow through the extension of state boundaries all the way to the Pacific Ocean. Instead, the ordinance stated that Americans were to settle the new land, exploit its resources, develop economically and politically and eventually form states on the same footing as the original colonies. The ordinance also forbade slavery and said that lands were not to be taken from the Native Americans. One promise was kept, the other was not.

The people who settled Ohio took to that task enthusiastically, and Cincinnati was the leader; it was the liveliest and fastest-growing settlement in the new territory. The city doesn't celebrate that part of its history very visibly. It's hard to preserve a sense of what the area was like when the first Cincinnatians arrived—the vastness of the wilderness. They said that the trees grew so close together a squirrel could cross the state without touching ground. Easterners started moving into this Ohio wilderness on flatboats. The settlers had either been given grants of land from the federal government for their service in the Revolutionary War, or they bought from land speculators who had their own federal grants. Marietta was the first settlement on the north side of the Ohio, followed

The Jolly Flatboaters, a painting by G.C. Bingham (1847) that shows early travel on the Ohio. *Courtesy of the Library of Congress.*

by three in the Cincinnati area. The founders of the small village they called Losantiville settled in 1788 and planted twenty acres of corn between where Broadway and Walnut Street are today. The founders of the town probably lived for the first few years on venison, turkey, cornbread, beans and squash. The first public eating and drinking space in Cincinnati was Griffin Yeatman's Square and Compass (the Masonic symbols), which was established in 1793 and overlooked the public landing.

In her book *In Meat We Trust*, historian Maureen Ogle traces how the earliest settlers of the United States developed a sense of entitlement when it came to meat. In the Old World, grazing land was scarce, and meat was a luxury, but in America, there was enough land and animals to eat meat every day. To Europeans, raising livestock was the highest use for land. So, in their minds, they had more claim to the land than the Native Americans, who didn't raise any animals—they only hunted and grew crops.

That was just one self-serving attitude that European immigrants had about Native Americans, of course, and it became part of a cycle

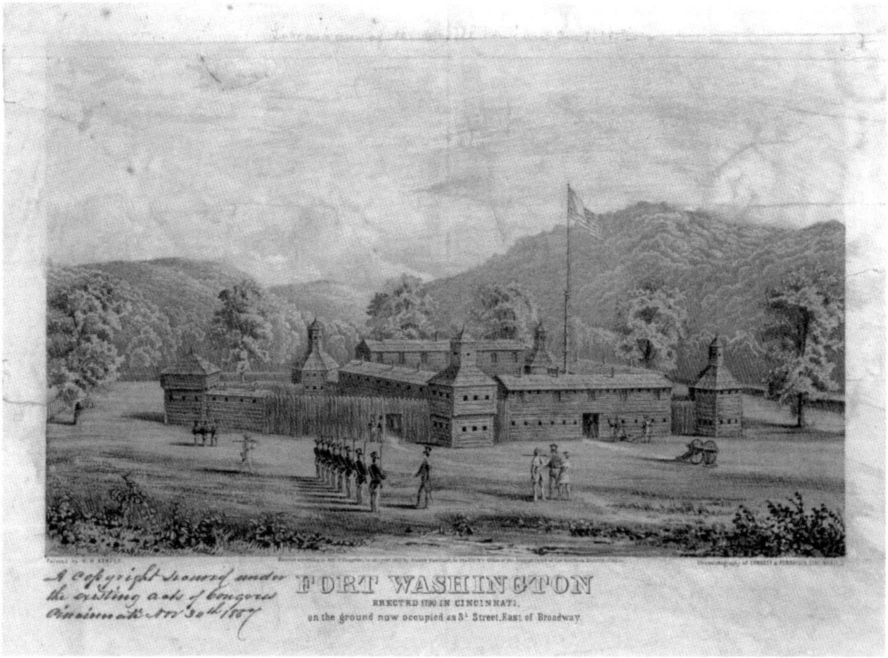

Fort Washington was built by the U.S. Army in 1789 to protect settlers in Cincinnati. *Courtesy of the Library of Congress.*

of distrust and hatred. When the English settlers' livestock trampled the Native Americans' crops, the natives killed the settlers' cattle and hogs in retribution. The cycle of attack and re-attack went on, and it was a struggle that the natives inevitably lost. Eventually, the Native Americans who had inhabited southwestern Ohio lost their land to livestock-raising Europeans. It's a shameful story that includes the common story of breaking of a treaty as soon as settlers wanted more land.

The federal government put its force behind making southeastern Ohio safe for white people. In 1789, Fort Washington was built in Losantiville to hold federal troops fighting the Shawnee. Some of the settlers stayed near the fort, while others moved to the upcountry and established stations, fort-like settlements with a stockade for protection and farms around it. After General Arthur St. Clair lost one battle with the Native Americans, George Washington gave the job to General "Mad Anthony" Wayne. After Wayne defeated a group of one thousand natives at the Battle of Fallen Timbers, the Greenville Treaty confined the Native Americans to the northwest corner of Ohio and whatever lands were to the west.

There's not much left in Cincinnati's food culture today that can be traced back to those early settlers or Native Americans. But corn, the crop that early settlers learned about from the natives, was the foundation for all of the city's following developments. The area around Cincinnati was good land for corn. When the natives finally had to give up their claim on the woods, the settlers spread north from the original Losantiville settlement and started farming. They cut down trees or girdled and burned them. By 1822, a visitor reported that "all the land in the immediate neighborhood of Cincinnati [was] without a tree on it." The settlers planted grains and gardens in the clearings, and corn was the most useful crop. The settlers ate it frequently in the form of pone, mush and cornbread. It could also be used to make whisky. But the best way to convert corn into cash was to feed it to hogs. Hogs were the perfect wilderness wealth-maker; they ate acorns and other foraged food in the woods, and they could kill the many poisonous snakes that vexed early farmers. The hogs were fed grain to fatten up, and the flesh of a hog took much better to preserving through smoking, pickling or salting than beef or poultry, so it could be sold and shipped to other areas in the expanding country. And unlike whisky or cornmeal, a hog could walk itself to market.

Cincinnati was where the hogs walked. New settlers were coming down the river, and the settlement grew quickly. By 1803, the city had 1,000 inhabitants; by 1810, it had 2,320. Five years later, the city's population had grown to 6,000. The first slaughterhouses in Cincinnati were established in 1810, and by 1811, the first steamboat had been built in Cincinnati. Only thirty years after its settlement, Cincinnati was the industrial leader of Ohio. "The manufactories of this new place are more diversified than extensive. An iron foundry, two breweries, several distilleries, a woolen mill, an oil mill, a glass house and a white lead factory seem to be the principal ones," said traveler James Flint in 1819.

But it was the meatpackers who became the most important workers in the city. The slaughterhouses were located in the middle of the city, on Deer Creek, a tributary of the Ohio River between downtown and Mount Adams. They were located, more or less, where Eggleston Avenue is now. At first, hogs were brought into town, slaughtered and trucked to the packing plants. These plants were run like factories, with "disassembly" lines that used conveyor systems for efficiency. Each worker did his part in killing, scalding and butchering the animals and packing the meat. In the 1820s, Cincinnati meatpackers processed thirty thousand hogs annually; by 1837, they were processing one hundred thousand hogs annually; and by the 1850s, they were processing more than four hundred thousand annually. The packing was done in rock salt, a method that was perfected by Richard Fosdick. The shoulders, which are fatty and able to be preserved, were packed into wooden barrels called butts. (This is where the term pork butt comes from.)

It must have been exciting to be part of a boomtown that was centered on the river. The city was the focal point of western migration. At first, only flatboats left the public landing, and they only went downstream, all the way to New Orleans. (You could take a flatboat downriver, but you'd have to walk back.) This established trade ties with the South, creating linkages and sympathies that became important later on. Then, steamboats allowed upriver travel as well. The first phase of the Miami-Erie Canal, from Cincinnati to Dayton, opened in 1829 and was expanded to Toledo in 1831. This canal allowed farmers north of Cincinnati to send goods to the city.

But the town was also dirty, unsanitary, even disgusting. Many visitors remarked, at the time, how Deer Creek was a stream of blood that emptied into the Ohio River and mixed with the city's drinking water. They also

A view of Cincinnati's canal, which connected the city to the Great Lakes. *Courtesy of the Cincinnati Public Library.*

told of how the streets were, at certain times of year, overrun with swine. They said hogs would get out of the way of carriages but not people and that they were impudent and filthy, though they admitted Cincinnati ham was very good. Isabella Lucy Bird, in her 1856 book, *The Englishwoman in America*, wrote:

> *I must not close this chapter without stating that the Queen City bears the less elegant name of Porkopolis; that swine, lean, gaunt and vicious looking, riot through her streets; and that, on coming out of the most splendid stores, one stumbles over these disgusting intruders. Cincinnati is the city of pigs.*

More frequently quoted is another Englishwoman named Fanny Trollope. A gentlewoman and the mother of English novelist Anthony Trollope, Fanny left a broke husband back home and came to Cincinnati in 1828 to see if she could get some kind of enterprise going. She built an elaborate store called Trollope's Bazaar that failed miserably. She was emphatically not impressed by the city, and she was particularly appalled by the presence of pigs and their slaughter. She later wrote in her book *Domestic Manners of Americans*:

> *When we had screwed our courage to the enterprise of mounting a certain noble-looking sugar-loaf hill, that promised pure air and a fine view, we found the brook we had to cross, at its foot, red with the stream from a pig slaughterhouse while our noses, instead of meeting the "thyme that loves the green hill's breast," were greeted by odours that I will not describe, and which I heartily hope my readers cannot imagine.*

However, it should be noted that this problem was not exclusive to Cincinnati. Eastern cities in the early 1900s had to deal with pigs in urban areas. At least they just ran through the streets in Cincinnati. In New York, they were kept in piggeries in residential areas, where they were useful as garbage processors.

Cincinnati was eventually shamed by the dirty business of hog slaughtering, and in the 1870s and 1880s, the meatpackers, slaughterhouses and stockyards moved west of town, to the Mill Creek Valley. It gave the packers better access to transportation networks, and it moved the nastiness out of the city a bit. The slaughterhouses simply dumped blood and waste into Mill Creek, which was already degraded by agriculture and industry—at least it was downriver of the intake for drinking water on the Ohio River. Meatpacking continued to be one of Cincinnati's

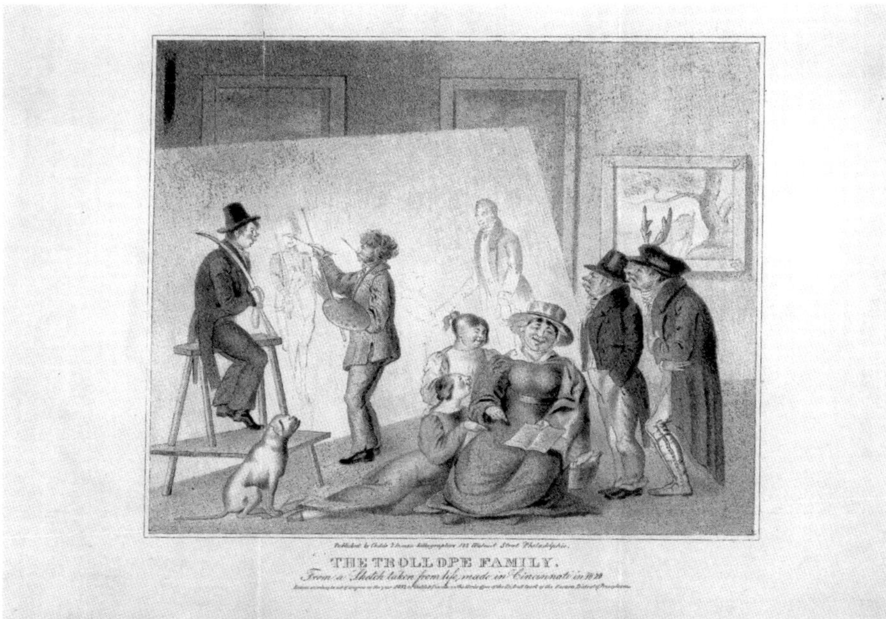

The Trollope Family: From a Sketch Taken from Life, Made in Cincinnati in 1829 (Childs & Inman, publisher), reflected what Cincinnatians thought of Fanny Trollope's criticisms of their town. *Courtesy of the Library of Congress.*

main industries throughout the rest of the nineteenth century and into the twentieth century, but Chicago surpassed Cincinnati as the country's meatpacking center starting in the 1870s. Chicago had bet on railroads (and beef), while Cincinnati thought steamboats would continue being sufficient. So, Chicago took over the problems of having a rough and bloody industry at its heart, but there continued to be a packing industry along Spring Grove Avenue for many years. Kahn's Meats was the largest meatpacking company on Spring Grove Avenue and in Ohio. Though they made beef and pork hot dogs, ham and other pork products, it was established by a Jewish immigrant named Elias Kahn, and it was carried on by his sons, Nathan, Albert, Louis and Eugene, and daughter, Matilda. It was out of business by 2006. Queen City Sausage is the last meat business standing in the old meatpacking district of Camp Washington.

Ironically, filthy meatpacking gave birth to clean soap making in Cincinnati. William Procter, an English store keeper and candle maker, and James A. Gamble, an Irish soap maker, were married to sisters in Cincinnati. They teamed up to form a candle and soap business, which were both, at the time, being made with animal fat or lard from hogs

Pigs hanging in the slaughterhouse of Kahn's Meats, which employed thousands of Cincinnatians over the years. *Courtesy of the* Cincinnati Enquirer.

and tallow from beef. Procter and Gamble started by making soap from animal fat, and the company went on to create Ivory and hundreds of other consumer products. Procter and Gamble became the world's largest advertiser and one of Cincinnati's wealthiest companies. So, those flying pigs were honoring more than Cincinnati's original industry—they are the patron saints of Tide, Crest and Crisco, too. The meatpackers had another profound effect on industries that followed it. They modeled innovative manufacturing processes, particularly the assembly line, in which each worker did their particular job on the line.

Pork packing wasn't the only industry in which Cincinnati led before the Civil War. While the pigs were being driven to the slaughterhouses, a remarkable man was creating the country's first winemaking industry.

3
CATAWBA WINE AND THE QUEEN CITY OF THE WEST

In 2016, on McMicken Street, at the foot of one of the hills that inspired Cincinnati's nickname City of Seven Hills, Kate MacDonald established an urban winery that she calls Skeleton Root. In the tasting room, leather couches flank a blown-up print of those hills, with grapevines growing up the slopes above the river. This is where I tasted her first bottling of Catawba wine after it had aged in oak barrels for three years.

Most Catawba wine is sweet. The Catawba is a native American grape, a relative of slip-skin Concords and other grapes that taste like grape juice or grape jelly. Because the grapes are actually quite low in sugar, most wineries that make a Catawba add a lot of sugar. Meier Winery, which has been making wine in Cincinnati's suburb of Silverton for over one hundred years, makes both a sweet white and sweet pink Catawba. But that's not what MacDonald was going for at all. She thinks it's possible, with careful winemaking techniques, to use such chilly weather and low-sugar grapes to make a nuanced and balanced wine. She makes wine from Norton and Isabella grapes, both of which are native, but the Catawba has a particularly special place in MacDonald's ambition. She has re-created the wine that was made in Cincinnati back when the city was the first center of American winemaking. She has gotten as close as possible to the wine that was made by Nicholas Longworth, who owned the vineyards depicted in the print on the wall.

Longworth was a New Jersey native who moved to Cincinnati in 1803, the year Ohio became a state and he turned twenty-one. Longworth had studied law, established a practice and set out to get rich. You can meet him at the Taft Museum, where his portrait hangs over a staircase. You'll see a note pinned to his sleeve like a modern Post-It Note and another fluttering to the floor. "His slovenly appearance and stentorian elocution were certainly anything but attractive," remembered Gorham Worth in his 1819 book, *Recollections of Cincinnati*. But as Worth said, he was "blest with untiring industry and the happiest assurance."

There is a story that Abraham Lincoln, who visited Longworth's house, mistook him for the gardener. Lincoln wasn't completely wrong, as Longworth was an accomplished horticulturist. He was interested in the scientific culture of strawberries and how he could turn them into an early cash crop for some Cincinnati farmers. Longworth also developed the first commercial black raspberry cultivar. He made his money, though, on real estate in a booming market. Cincinnati was growing; it was starting to fill in the basin that is formed by those flanking hills. Just like a modern-day celebrity, Longworth then invested in winemaking.

In the 1820s, Cincinnati's drinks of choice were cider, whisky or fortified wine. Longworth thought something a little lighter and less alcoholic was called for, and he set out to make wine. He tried cultivating vinifera grapes, or those noble varieties from Europe, like Chardonnay or Cabernet, but they succumbed to disease. So, he adopted the hardier Catawba, a native grape crossed with a European grape, and by 1840, he was making a decent wine. One reason he succeeded was his collaboration with one immigrant group that went on to shape so much of Cincinnati's history: the Germans. They were the first significant immigrant group to the United States, and some of them had started settling in Cincinnati almost since the city's beginning. (Martin Baum, one of the city's early mayors, was a German immigrant who built the house that Longworth eventually bought; it is now the Taft Museum.) Many of these recent immigrants knew about wine and about cultivating grapes. Their experiences on the Rhine translated well to the slopes of the Ohio. So, the German farmers grew the grapes, while Longworth controlled the winemaking process, including the barreling, bottling and marketing, himself.

The Germans weren't just helpful at making the wine; they also liked to drink it. It was a light, dry white wine, reminiscent of the hock wines of the Rhone Valley, and it was served in taverns and gardens throughout the city.

The mansion Nicholas Longworth bought from Martin Baum in 2016. It is now the Taft Museum of Art. *Courtesy of Carol M. Highsmith, Library of Congress.*

Not everyone took to it, though. Frances Trollope wrote, "The very best of it was miserable stuff." But then, Trollope never had many good things to say about her time in Cincinnati.

The wine was also not what most Americans were used to drinking—too light and dry. But then, Longworth made it sparkle. It was an accident that created his ultimate success. In 1842, when some of the wine went through an unintended second fermentation in the bottle, a sparkling, Champagne-like version of the wine was created. So, he decided to re-create the sparkling wine on purpose, and he hired a French expert to help him. The expert unfortunately drowned in the Ohio River on his way to his new job, so Longworth had to hire another one. The new wine was a hit. What made the original wine a hard sell was its aromatic but dry qualities, but those qualities are perfect for a sparkling wine. It became popular throughout the country and was even exported to Europe.

In 1857, Longworth sent a case of the sparkling Catawba to famous Cincinnati-born sculptor Hiram Power, who was then living in Italy. Power wrote back to thank him and to say that his aristocratic friend the Marquis Ponciattica would like to buy a barrel. He also sent some to the poet Henry Wadsworth Longfellow, who then wrote "Ode to Catawba," a poem about Longworth's wines. It's not one of his best poems; it's more of an elaborate thank-you note that popularized Cincinnati's most genteel nickname: the Queen City. Its last two verses:

While pure as a spring
Is the wine I sing,
And to praise it, one needs but name it;
For Catawba wine
Has need of no sign,
No tavern-bush to proclaim it.

And this Song of the Vine,
This greeting of mine,
The winds and the birds shall deliver
To the Queen of the West,
In her garlands dressed,
On the banks of the Beautiful River.

The winemaking project in Cincinnati lasted for a few decades, but the Civil War left no one to tend the grapes, and diseases struck the vines. Longworth died in 1863. By 1870, the southeastern Ohio wine industry was basically gone, but the history of the industry became one of those "firsts" from the past that Cincinnati can claim proudly.

Longworth left a paper trail. "He took notes and kept good records," MacDonald said. "That's what has led me on this weird path." MacDonald, a West Side native, trained and worked as an engineer. Her interest in wine was sparked when she lived in the Finger Lakes wine region of New York. She got her first experience in winemaking at Valley Vineyards in Morrow, east of Cincinnati. After this experience, she quit her job and went to Napa Valley, where she worked at Lewis Cellars, which makes classic California Cabernet and Chardonnay. While she was there, MacDonald started learning the American wine story. "When I found out that American wine production started in Cincinnati, it blew my mind. Why did I leave Cincinnati to make wine?" she asked herself. So, she came back home and opened Skeleton Root.

She started buying locally raised vinifera grapes, including Cabernet Franc and Seyval Blanc, which do well in Cincinnati. In 2014, she contracted with a Kentucky grower for those grapes, but the polar vortex hit that winter and brought with it arctic temperatures for weeks in a row. The grower lost about half of her crop to the cold weather. The half of

"Corking bottles in Mr. Longworth's cellars," from *Harpers Weekly*, 1858. *Courtesy of the Library of Congress.*

the crop that was unharmed was made up of Norton grapes, a native American variety. This changed MacDonald's direction. She still makes wines from some vinifera grapes, but she's really hooked on other oddball American grapes, including Isabella, Regent and especially Norton, which she has made several red wines from.

This all eventually led to MacDonald Catawba. No one had made a dry wine from this grape for so long that she had to figure out how to do it by using Longworth's writing and notes as clues. Like him, she fermented it in oak casks on the lees, which contributes creaminess and body. She's facing many of the same challenges that Longworth did—both in winemaking and public acceptance. She knew it was hard to make a sophisticated wine from Catawba, and she knew that even if she did, people might not want it. "There has always been a view that American grapes can't make wine to rival Europe. People do think we're crazy using these grapes that no one has heard of, but if you come to every new wine expecting it to taste like something you've already had, you'll never find anything new to like."

Each year, MacDonald tries to make her Catawba less "bitey" by aging it, and she will not stop until she is satisfied and excited by it. Now, she has created a "pet nat," or a naturally sparkling wine, in order to get closer to her model.

The first bottling of Skeleton Root Winery's Heritage Catawba wine. *Courtesy of the* Cincinnati Enquirer *and Cara Owsley.*

Longworth advertised his wine as Pure Nature Catawba to distinguish it from the manipulated and fortified wines of the time. That made him seem like a visionary, a man who anticipated the twenty-first-century interest in natural wines, pure local foods and knowing where food and drinks come from. MacDonald loves to think of her Catawba being served in local restaurants—a heritage regional wine paired with the region's heritage foods. Just think of the wine being paired with a smoked pork chop and sauerkraut or a plate of fatty sausages. (Those sausages were the signature dish of Cincinnati once the German compatriots of Longworth's workers began arriving in great numbers in the late 1840s.)

4

THE GERMANS ARRIVE IN OVER-THE-RHINE

Oktoberfest season starts early in Cincinnati; it's the only way to give each festival its own weekend. The first festival is hosted by the Germania Society at their park in late August. Main Strasse Village in Covington, Kentucky, puts on their festival in early September. The Donauschwaben Society's festival takes place in early October. There are many smaller festivals in the local neighborhoods and churches during the season as well.

The big festival is Oktoberfest Zinzinnati, and it is held in late September, just as it is in Munich. At the downtown event, which attracts half a million people and is second in the world in size only to Munich, many men deck themselves out in lederhosen, gingham shirts and Bavarian hats, while women put on their complete dirndl outfits—or possibly their abbreviated and exaggeratedly sexy dirndl outfits. German folk dancing groups entertain, and German bands' oom-pah versions of "The Beer Barrel Polka" and "Sweet Caroline" blend together as visitors walk from stall to stall, eating wursts, schnitzel, huge cream puffs that are hard for even two people to finish, potato pancakes, pretzels and strudel that is all downed with lots of Oktoberfest beer. It's fun and German-ish, even if it's a little narrow and stereotyped.

At the smaller fests, which are run by German heritage organizations, the crowd is smaller, and the food is a bit more homemade and traditional. At the Germania Society, there are Oktoberfest chickens rotating over charcoal fires, and plate dinners are served inside. In a picnic pavilion, couples of all ages dance to polkas and waltzes. The Donauschwaben

Mr. and Mrs. Martin Lohs of Kenwood dressed in German garb for an event in 1951. *Courtesy of the* Cincinnati Enquirer *and Allan Kain.*

members pit-roast pork and chicken and serve stuffed cabbage, goulash, tortes and pastries on the side.

These events can feel kitschy, especially when a C-list celebrity or local sports figure leads the downtown crowd in "the world's largest chicken dance," but they are expressions of genuine ethnic identity. About 25 percent of Cincinnatians have German heritage, according to a 2017 Census Bureau estimate. For the rest of us, German food isn't hard to like, and it lends itself well to this kind of street situation, unifying everyone—except, perhaps for the super-smelly and more divisive limburger cheese and onion sandwiches, which are still on the menu in a few stands.

The earliest founders of Cincinnati were mostly Protestants from New Jersey. In 1830, Cincinnati's population was made up mostly of native-born Americans from all regions of the country; only 5 percent of the city's population were born in Germany. Germans were the earliest group of non-British immigrants to come to the United States in large numbers. Many came after hearing that the United States was "*das land der unbegrenzten möglichkeiten*" (a land of unlimited possibilities). Friedrich Gerstaecker called Cincinnati in particular "the El Dorado of the German emigrant." Cincinnati was a boomtown where many of the skilled laborers and craftsmen among these German immigrants could find jobs. Cincinnati was building steamboats, making carriages and bottling whisky. Some immigrants became farmers, others became brewers and others worked in trades that were the basis for future printing and machine tool industries. Some were bakers, and many found work in meat processing.

By 1840, 30 percent of Cincinnati's population was German. By 1850, there were thirty thousand Germans living in Cincinnati from many German states, including Bavaria, Württemberg and the Rhineland. They were Catholic, Lutheran, German Reformed and Jewish It's common to hear people say that Germans gave Cincinnati its signature conservatism, but the first Germans were a force of change. "The German refugees brought a fresh, liberal point of view that tempered the Presbyterian stringency on the one hand and the boomtown irregularity on the other," wrote the author of the *WPA Guide to Cincinnati*, a lively introduction to Cincinnati history that was published in 1943 as a project of the Works Progress Administration.

Attitudes toward the Germans were not as negative as the attitudes that were directed toward some subsequent immigrant groups—at least at first. There were many Germans, often Protestant, who were seen as high-culture, associated with classical music and literature. Germans were acknowledged to be hard working, but there was also the image of the drunk Dutchman

"Nightfall on the Ohio, Cincinnati, Ohio." Steamboats continued to be used on the Ohio River into the twentieth century, but they were in decline when this photograph was taken between 1900 and 1920. *Courtesy of the Detroit Publishing Company photograph collection, Library of Congress.*

(more likely Catholic) who was fat, jovial and both ate and drank too much. This image was later held against the Germans during Prohibition and, of course, World War I. The *WPA Guide* described Germans as great eaters, "having meat and potatoes three times a day," eating "tripe and pigs' feet, hasenpfeffer [rabbit cooked in red wine], sauerkraut, potato pancakes, cinnamon kuchen and smoked sausages."

Another glimpse onto German tables can be found in Charlotte Pieper's novel *Wooden Shoe Hollow*, which is about an enclave of German farmers in Winton Place in 1913. They live modestly but eat well. The characters in the detailed novel butcher a hog in the fall and make mettwurst with mustard seeds and coarse black pepper. They have bacon, roast beef, creamed peas, "snippled" green beans, mashed potatoes, zwieback, sausage sandwiches, a wash basket full of sandwiches at a wedding and roast goose at Christmas. They also have plum kuchen, coconut pie, stollen, doughnuts, jelly rolls, "thick egg pies" with cinnamon and nutmeg and lots of coffee. One of the girls in the novel goes to work for a "Yankee" family and comes back to her friends, bemoaning how her employers eat "like sparrows."

> *"Do you know they eat only three meals a day? And no potatoes for breakfast? Or meat either!"*
>
> *"No morning lunch even?" Rosie gasped. "How can they stand it?"*
>
> *"I don't know, but they do. Honest. Afternoon lunch is what I missed most."*

Germans loved the good things in life, like music, art, beer and food, and they were proud of being German. They were great joiners of organizations; they joined singing clubs, brass bands and Turnerverein societies, where they cultivated physical activities like gymnastics and fencing. Most of Cincinnati's German immigrants crowded into a neighborhood called Over-the-Rhine. This neighborhood was north of the city's downtown, on the other side of the Miami-Erie Canal. Going over the canal was metaphorically seen as crossing the Rhine into a German world.

I was surprised to get insight into Over-the-Rhine when I visited the Tenement Museum in New York City. One of the tours offered there is of the first-floor business space in their building on Orchard Street. It re-creates how the room may have looked during the time that the Lower East Side was called Kleindeutschland, or Little Germany. It was called this during the 1830s and 1840s, the same time period in which Germans first moved to Cincinnati and created Over-the-Rhine. The architecture is similar as well; the narrow row houses were connected for a whole city block, with three stories up and one down.

The snug little tavern on the first floor, which was the size of a living room, is where the proprietor served beer and offered food from the homeland. A back room served as political meeting space, and one small kitchen served both the business and the family, who were confined to one bedroom in the back. Over-the-Rhine was an extremely crowded neighborhood. Before 1870, it was the most crowded community in the United States, with thirty-two thousand people living in every square mile. There were scores of small taverns, bakeries and butchers, along with breweries, biergartens and cafés, in the neighborhood. The butchers sold a greater variety of meat than we eat today, including kidneys, tripe, pigs' head, feet and a wide variety of sausages; they probably each reflected the geographic origin of the butcher.

Turnerleben, a gathering of Turner Societies where Germans met for athletic activities around 1831 or 1832. *Courtesy of the Public Library of Cincinnati and Hamilton County.*

Sausages became an emblem of the Germans and eventually of Cincinnati. Non-Germans eyed "wursts" suspiciously, thinking of everything they might contain. There are quite a few stories from the *Enquirer* in the 1880s that detail illness or death from eating bad sausages, and there are nervous stories about meat from horses, cats and dogs being used in the sausages. One of the poorest, rowdiest neighborhoods in Cincinnati was called Sausage Row. Sausages were linked with Cincinnati enough by 1869 to inspire a mercilessly satirical article in the *Chicago Tribune* about Cincinnatians:

> *They are a primitive race, easy-going and sedate.... They are great sausage-eaters. They have them for breakfast, dinner and supper, and for dessert. If they want to go to the deuce, they go not on champagne or whiskey or anything else, but on sausages. In this and this only are they original. When they travel, they always carry sausages. A native of Porkopolis would as soon go without his clothes as go without sausages in his pockets.*

In *Pioneers of Night Life on Vine Street*, a collection of newspaper stories about the saloons and entertainments of Over-the-Rhine in the decades before

Dave Lindner boiling sausages at Avril & Son after stuffing them by hand and curing and smoking them in 1981. *Courtesy of the* Cincinnati Enquirer *and Allan Kain.*

Prohibition, there is a story of a man named Bader who brings sausages to a bar run by a Mr. Pels and asks him to cook them.

> *Presently, the appetizing flavor came floating out from the kitchen. To the uninitiated, the odor would have seemed all right, but those old war horses, who had battled with sausages from their earliest days, knew better. Bader got up and walked back to the kitchen, where he found Pels busily poking a fork into the "linked sweetness."... Without saying a word, Bader walked back into the café. Actually, the tears were rolling down his cheeks. The sacrilege had moved him profoundly.*

Wienerwursts became an important part of Cincinnati life in the 1880s, when the wienerwurst men began to operate. These were men and young boys who carried boxes of the wienerwursts around to saloons or workplaces. A small lamp in the box kept the wienerwursts hot, and they'd serve them on a slice of rye with horseradish. An *Enquirer* article from 1881 describes a reporter's encounter with a small boy selling wienerwursts at 2:00 a.m. The reporter asked the boy if he could follow him to the factory where his wieners were made; the sausage makers there told him that three parts beef and one part pork went into the sausages, which were made with a mechanical chopper and mixer. The reporter asked if dogs or cats ever went into the sausage, betraying that prejudice, and the sausage maker responded with an emphatic, "No!" The reporter went away satisfied that the best cuts of meat went into the wieners.

Cincinnati was known as Porkopolis for processing meat, not for eating it. The city's carnivorous habits were affected more by the meat-heavy German menu. Sausages are still a big deal in Cincinnati. At the Reds' Great American Ballpark, visitors won't find just hot dogs. The park also offers brats and metts, the city's summertime tradition. Small neighborhood butchers still live on in Cincinnati. When Germans prospered and moved out of the dense, often unhealthy Over-the-Rhine neighborhood, many gravitated to the West Side. On that side of town, where traditions die hard, there are many neighborhood stores that still cut their own meat, make their own sausages, smoke hams and sell pork chops. Wassler Meats, Humbert's, Meiners and Bridgetown Finer Meats all serve their neighborhoods with butchers who are at the ready to sell customers quality meat. One store downtown, Avril-Bleh Meats on Court Street, stands out for its variety of shop-made products.

5

THE MEATS WE EAT

In 2010, Senate restaurant opened on Vine Street in the new Gateway Quarter of Over-the-Rhine. Its young owner and chef from Chicago, Daniel Wright, served up-to-date dishes, like a flavor bomb of a poutine made with short rib gravy and mussels in a chermoula sauce and an arugula salad, but the restaurant quickly became known for hot dogs. Its fancy hot dogs, like the croque madame with béchamel, local ham and a poached egg on a brioche bun, or the Lindsay Lohan with goat cheese, caramelized onions, bacon and "tons of drama," became popular.

Senate was just the beginning of a boom of restaurants and bars that had a lot of success on Vine Street north of Central Parkway. After a few years, Wright wanted to start using a higher-quality hot dog, something custom made with a distinctive flavor. So, he called Len Bleh of Avril-Bleh Meat Market, which was a few blocks from the restaurant on the other side of Central Parkway. The chef from the trendy restaurant and the owner of a heritage meat market that was founded in 1894 got together, and over the course of six months, they came up with just the right all-beef dog. Avril-Bleh started making the recipe exclusively for Senate. By 2014, they were making four thousand hot dogs a month.

This was a big order, but it was nothing beyond the capability of a butcher shop that still makes more than thirty products for its butcher case, including a wide variety of sausages and lunch meats, like pickle loaf, pickled pigs' feet and more than one kind of ham. All of the shop's meat is made in a narrow building that's held these wonders since the 1920s. There is something so

A customer chooses from the case at Avril-Bleh Meats in 2019. *Courtesy of the* Cincinnati Enquirer *and Liz Dufour.*

very Cincinnati about Avril's. The shop tends to business the old way, which is to say the hard way. Their products are as solid as a BMW, but they're not glamorous. And there's very little marketing or merchandising to bring attention to the shop or make it look like anything but what it is: a butcher shop where regular people come to get their meat.

Anton Avril, an immigrant from Germany's Rhineland, started selling meat from a wagon in the Findlay and Court Street public markets in 1894. Avril made all his products at home in the West End and became known as "the boiled ham king." After his death in 1926, his son Ferdy opened the store on Court Street, next door to its current location. His sons Ferd and Werneth were both musicians; they played drums and trumpet in both college and the army, and it looked like they might move on from the family business. But by the late 1950s, they had taken over the shop, doing things the way their father had. Their employee Len Bleh bought the shop in 1998, at a time when there wasn't much going on in that part of downtown or in Over-the-Rhine.

Len Bleh has been a faithful steward of the tradition ever since, but he has done a lot to bring things up to date. He still adds a dash of tomato juice to the tiny links of breakfast sausage because that's what the Avril brothers taught him—although he's not quite sure what it does for the final product. But he's also moved into supplying restaurants, hosting sausage classes and marketing on social media. An excellent introduction to Avril's is the grill it sets up on the sidewalk in the summer. From there, the butcher shop sells grilled metts and brats and Italian and Polish sausage (never poked with a fork, of course). The big fat sausages snap when you bite into them; they're juicy, salty and full of real meat flavor and a hit of what distinguishes that sausage: smoke, mustard seeds or garlic.

The first few times I went to Avril's, I didn't really appreciate it. I just saw a long glass case filled with a lot of pale sausages, some cuts of beef and cheese. The bagged white bread, mustards and potato chips for sale seemed commonplace. I was used to buying meat at a self-service grocery store before I moved to Cincinnati, so the first thing I really noticed was all the men working there who all knew what they were doing. There's a long tradition of trained butchers in Cincinnati, and they're all knowledgeable and expert at efficiently wrapping meat in white butcher's paper, weighing it, labeling it and asking what else you want. I soon got an education in sausages, and all those pale tubes began to distinguish themselves from one another. I would take my father gifts of their homemade pickle loaf, olive loaf or headcheese, the kind of thing that will probably be last enjoyed by his generation. It's not often you get an artisanal olive loaf. Sometimes, I buy their dried beef and make the best chipped beef gravy on toast possible. I've also bought an Easter ham there, smoked but still needing further baking. There is no water added and no fluid injected. Their liverwurst is good enough to serve as a pâté.

While Ferd and Werneth Avril and Len Bleh kept on making and serving tradition without thinking of trends, the rest of the culinary world was circling back around to their kind of butchery and sausage-making. Snout-to-tail cooking, charcuterie plates, better sausages and unusual cuts of meat all became part of the gastronomic conversation in the United States. Carbs became the enemy and fat became the friend. Avril's still serves its faithful, aging customers, but it has a new influx of fans, younger people who have come to appreciate and understand a more old-fashioned approach to meat. Avril's has endured.

Senate isn't the only restaurant that serves Avril's products; the shop makes a bier baron sausage for Moerlein Lager House on the river, as well as sausages and ground beef for Zips, the beloved burger restaurant on Mount Lookout Square, and Texas sausages for local barbecue restaurants. I've been to the shop's sausage making class that's about understanding what goes into Avril's sausages (and an opportunity for lots of sausage jokes). Each one is a variation on what meat goes into it (some are made with beef, but they are mostly made from pork from Indiana), how finely it's ground, whether it's skinless (encased in a collagen coating that is cut off after cooking the sausage) or made in natural casing (encased in a cleaned pork or lamb intestine), whether it's cooked or fresh, smoked or not and the spice mix unique to that sausage. Avril's also sells a couple of different kinds of goetta (with and without onion because Ferd didn't like onion) and smoked oatmeal rings, a cousin of goetta. This brings us to the subject of Cincinnati's favorite, unique breakfast food.

Goetta

It's a Saturday morning at Eckerlin Meats in Findlay Market, and customers are packed two or three deep in the narrow space in front of the meat counter. Behind the counter, five or six men crisscross each other as they fill orders: one for tri-tip or flat iron steak, one for bacon and smoked pork, one for chicken rolled with prosciutto and peppers, ready to grill, and many, many for goetta. *Regular or peppered?* they ask. *How thick?* And customers use a thumb and finger to show whether they want it thick so that it will cook up crisp on the outside with a creamy inside or thin so that it can cook up good and crunchy.

It's pronounced "get-uh," or, if you're like a minority of native Cincinnatians, "gut-uh." This funny-looking breakfast meat is an emblem of Cincinnati, of huge nostalgic value for natives. It is now embraced as one of the city's quirkiest food products. Since it is almost aggressively non-glamorous, it's not surprising that goetta never caught on anywhere else. It's a pale gray loaf with a bumpy texture that is made from equal parts steel-cut oats, known in Cincinnati as pinhead oats, and meat (usually pork and beef), and it is cooked for hours and molded into a loaf. It's then sliced and fried in a pan until little bumps of oat start to splutter and pop and the slice turns a beautiful deep brown, ready to slide onto a breakfast plate.

Goetta has traditionally been used as a breakfast meat next to a couple of fried eggs, maybe with a touch of maple syrup or ketchup on it. It has a pleasant texture and really does have a full serving of whole grain. It ranges from rich and fatty to quite lean, and its spicing can include cloves, herbs and onions—spices reminiscent of sausage. It's listed on the menu at restaurants that specialize in breakfast and home cooking, usually as one of the choices for breakfast meat. You can also eat a huge slab of it in an

There are two goetta festivals in Greater Cincinnati; this one is in Covington's Mainstrasse. *Courtesy of the* Cincinnati Enquirer.

omelet any time—day or night—at the Anchor Grill in Covington, Cincinnati's neighbor in Northern Kentucky. The Anchor is a dive bar that is open twenty-four hours a day, so goetta has soaked up its share of late-night binges and morning hangovers. Price Hill Chili and the Colonial Cottage in Northern Kentucky are among other restaurants that feature goetta prominently on their menus.

Goetta's origins are not exactly clear, but it's certainly German-American. Dann Woellert, the local food history blogger, has traced the genealogy of all grain-and-meat sausages from Europe in his book *Cincinnati Goetta.* The meat has a relative in Pennsylvania scrapple, a similar dish that uses cornmeal instead of oats. In other parts of Ohio, there are similar creations called grits or grutze. There's something similar, though it is smoked, from Hanover, Germany, called knipp. Cincinnatians who travel to Scotland and try haggis often note a certain similarity. Anywhere that humble people needed to mix some grains with the odds and ends of meat, you're likely to find something similar to goetta.

Traditionally, goetta was made at home and eaten in the cool and cold months. Even in the 1980s, Avril's only made goetta in the winter. Some people get a craving for it then, when a hearty breakfast is appropriate. But it's now available year-round. It's a Cincinnati tradition that the city has hung onto, even though sausage or bacon are the more mainstream choices. But goetta remained strictly regional and personal. No one thought to tout it beyond the 513 or 859 area codes. Cincinnatians liked it, but there was no reason to bring it to anyone else's attention. But in the last twenty years, it's become a matter of hometown pride. As people have become more interested in unique and regional foods, goetta has become at least interestingly quirky if not almost hip.

The re-positioning of goetta started with Glier's, a goetta-making company in Covington, Kentucky, just across the river from downtown Cincinnati. It was founded as a meat shop by Robert Glier in the 1940s, when he got home from World War II. In the 1960s, Glier moved the shop into an old Bavarian Brewing building in Covington and began producing goetta in bulk. It's the most commercially successful goetta on the market; it's packaged in cylindrical chubs that can be found at any grocery store in the Cincinnati area. Dan Glier, Robert's son and the current owner, experimented with different versions of goetta, including a lower-fat turkey product, beef goetta and spicy goetta. In 2015, the shop debuted bacon goetta. Around 1998, Glier and his marketing director, Mark Balasa, started marketing the product more aggressively, and they came up with goetta links and burgers. In 2002, the brand started hosting a goetta festival, where they would invite vendors to make up new products with goetta. Thus, goetta mac and cheese, goetta burritos and goetta potato skins were born. Goetta fudge may have been going too far. In my opinion, goetta's best trait is its crispness when it's fried. Anything that uses it without frying it first doesn't work nearly as well.

Today, visitors will come across restaurants using goetta in all kinds of ways, like goetta poutine or as a topping for hamburgers. Trotta's Pizza on the West Side pioneered using goetta as a pizza topping. Yat Ka Mein, a Chinese noodle restaurant in Oakley, sometimes serves their goetta fried rice as a special, and Mimi's Eggrolls in Findlay Market, which was owned by a Thai family and generally specializes in Thai-style egg rolls, used to make a monster goetta egg roll.

But even traditional goetta, served simply, ranges widely in flavor and texture. I once thought I had tried goetta from every independent butcher in Greater Cincinnati, but when I published a list, I still got calls about places I'd missed. Each one had its own personality. Some shops cook the oatmeal and meat until it's very soft, with a pastier, more homogenized texture. Others keep more texture difference between the grain and meat, making it a little more breakfast-sausage-like. The spicing varies widely, too, from some that are onion and thyme–heavy to others that taste more of clove.

Trying every kind is a completely doable quest for any Cincinnatian. If you grew up with your mother's or neighborhood butcher's, you probably aren't in the market for a new brand. But if you're new in town and want to establish your local bona fides, take a pleasant few weeks driving around town—the West Side especially—and conduct taste trials at breakfast. Everyone should have their own personal brand of goetta and be ready to defend it.

Brats and Metts

There isn't much left of Porkopolis. Down along Spring Grove Avenue, Kahn's finally was bought by Consolidated Food and then closed for good in 2006. Only one meatpacking company survives: Queen City Sausage, which is owned by Elmer Hensler, who's been in the meat business since he was twelve years old. In 1965, he opened Queen City Sausage with two partners; at that time, there were at least forty similar meat plants. Now, both the partners and the local competitors are all gone. Hensler once gave me a tour of his chilly, spotless sausage plant and introduced me to German emulsifying machines, the sausage stuffing process, secret spice mixes and smoking rooms.

Hensler, who was born in 1930, continued to run the business, even expanding it into his nineties; Queen City still makes a wide variety of traditional Cincinnati favorites. "I haven't beat anyone out of a penny in forty-six years," said Elmer for a story in 2011. At that time, he was eighty-two years old and had no plans to retire; he was busy raising the profile of his heritage company, starting a Queen City meats festival and marketing his natural-casing sausages to the new enthusiasts of grilling. He was competing with cheaper products by maintaining his meat's quality. (Mark Balasa, who started the goetta festival with Glier's, then came to Queen City Sausage to help them boost their image.) Hensler's plant is a meticulously clean and up-to-date facility that is staffed mostly by immigrants from Mexico. The products still reflect its German heritage. The company makes goetta, Leona, knockwurst and Dutch loaf. The company's brats and metts are the best-selling sausages in Cincinnati, and they are the official brat and mett of the Cincinnati Reds.

If a Milwaukee Brewers fan came to a game at Great American Ballpark, they'd be a little surprised by the brats that are served. In Milwaukee, and to most Americans, a brat is a big, coarsely ground fresh sausage that's grilled and eaten with beer. Not in Cincinnati. This city's brats are cousins of Munich's weisswurst; they are pale sausages that are either smoothly emulsified in a natural casing or kept skinless. And metts, at least by the name, are an only-in-Cincinnati thing. In Germany, there's something called mettwurst, a spreadable soft sausage, but Cincinnati's metts are smoked pork sausages that are delicious grilled. Together, they form Cincinnati's standard summer grill-out menu. A good mett is several times tastier than a standard hot dog. They're smoky and juicy and great with mustard, kraut or, most traditionally, horseradish. The spice levels range from mild to spicy to super-hot.

Cincinnati brats are a little harder to like because they're much milder in flavor, as they are not smoked. They're hard to grill because they split and burn easily. I find that they take to poaching and steaming much better because of their more delicate texture and flavor. Treated carefully, they are delicate and delicious. Steaming them in sauerkraut is perfect. Brats and metts come in skinless and natural casing varieties. The natural casing is a more traditional choice, obviously, and they give a much more satisfying sort of explosion when you bite into them.

Visitors will find house-made brats and metts in quite a few local butchers. Many shops also have a Hamilton mett on the menu. There's a theory that there was a "hemel" or "hamlet" mett and that the residents of Hamilton County just substituted that for the original name. Len Bleh says it's just a variation on metts that each butcher defines for themselves, but it is regarded as special.

A very different kind of mett is made by the parishioners of Fleming Road United Church of Christ, which incorporated the congregation of a

Ferd Avril checking sausages that had been cured for two days and were smoked and boiled in 1981. *Courtesy of the* Cincinnati Enquirer *and Allan Kain.*

church started by the German farmers and greenhouse keepers of Wooden Shoe Hollow, near Spring Grove Cemetery. Every year, the church finds someone to donate an apple tree that can be cut down, split and used for a fire to smoke sausages. The men gather in the church kitchen to chop and stuff the sausages, then smoke them in a portable smokehouse. The sausages are more coarsely ground than butchers' metts. They are a bit drier, but they are lovely and smoky and are served with sauerkraut, green beans, mashed potatoes and applesauce in the church's fellowship hall.

Other sausages that can be found at Cincinnati butcher shops include the extra-chubby knockwurst, which is a garlic sausage; bierwurst, which is made with a bit of beer; yard sausage, which is like a mett but in a long continuous cylinder; tiny links; and, in the spring, slender bockwurst, which is made with bock beer and is a must at the annual Bockfest. Several butchers also smoke their own hams.

Ham

A New York grocer told an *Enquirer* reporter in 1882 that "the finest cured hams in the world—certainly in this country—are the carefully cured grades by certain packers in Cincinnati." The John C. Roth Packing Company advertised its sugar-cured ham as "perfection in cure, highest attained on Earth." Those "certain packers" are not in business any longer, and since Kahn's shut down, Cincinnati no longer makes hams in large quantities. But a few people keep up the Cincinnati tradition, so it's possible to buy a local ham that is made with care. Avril's makes both a baked ham and a boiled ham; both are smoked in the shop's in-house smoker. Another local hammery—if that's the right word—is Sky Haven. The shop has been around since 1955 and is located in an old farmhouse on the edge of Mount Airy Forest. Ed Dreyer inherited the shop from his father and still makes hams by hand every day, using an old smoking chamber and very little technology. Many commercial hams are injected with brine to make them cheaper, which also makes them rubberier in texture. Some hams have more than 15 percent of their weights in water added. Sky Haven and some other hams are classified as "ham with natural juices," meaning they have only 7 to 8 percent of their weights in water added. The Avril's version is the same.

Then, there's a kind of ham you won't find, at least by its Cincinnati name, anywhere else: cottage ham. Ham and green beans cooked until the

Above: Smoked hams in the cold storage rooms of the H.H. Meyer Co. after a fourteen-hour smoke in 1960. *Courtesy of the McHale Studio.*

Right: Ed Dreyer wrapping a ham before hanging it on the racks at Sky Haven Farms in Mount Airy. *Courtesy of the* Cincinnati Enquirer *and Amanda Davidson.*

beans are soft and silky-textured is a common dish across the Appalachians and upper South. Many Cincinnatians cook this dish up in crockpots, often with the addition of potatoes, for gatherings and traditional family suppers. The kind of ham that is used in this dish varies, but in Cincinnati, the meat is usually a cottage ham. That's the local name for a smoked pork shoulder, so it's not technically a ham at all but a fist-sized knob of dense meat that is smoked and very firm. Bluegrass Meats from Kentucky makes these hams, as does Avril's, Queen City Sausage and Wassler's Meats on the West Side. But no one makes them quite like Stehlin's, a butcher in Colerain Township.

In fact, there are very few places like Stehlin's anywhere. In October, the traditional meat processing time of year, Stehlin's gears up to accept a weekly delivery of at least twenty local hogs that are grown to their standards. The hogs walk into the back of the building on Colerain Avenue on their own four feet and leave as chops, roasts, sausages and goetta for the butcher store in the front. It's a living Porkopolis, though it is far more modern and hygienic today. Stehlin's has been doing this since 1913, plugging along as everything around the shop has changed, including the ever-more-stringent government regulations, big changes in what people eat and how they cook and competition from a huge, centralized meat industry. "I guess we're just stubborn," said Denny Stehlin, one of the owners. "There used to be a lot of outfits like us. Most of them have given up."

Grandpa John Stehlin, who was always known as Butch, was driving animals to the stockyards in downtown Cincinnati when a flood closed all of the slaughterhouses. He stopped in at a local farm, slaughtered the animals himself and sold the meat to his neighbors. Since then, the Stehlins have learned the craft from their elders. "I could skin a steer by myself by the time I was fourteen," said Denny.

The family likes an old-style pork cushioned with fat; it's chubbier than most pork you buy in a supermarket, because pigs started being bred lean over health concerns starting in the mid-twentieth century. The shop works with local farmers who can supply what it's looking for. The popularity of low and slow barbecue means that the shop gets a lot of customers for pork butts, where a little extra fat means more luscious meat. And some people still buy the shop's sausage that is called Johnny in the bag. It's a sausage made of pork, blood and cornmeal. "I thought that one would just die off," said Denny's cousin Dick, another owner. "But there are still people who grew up with it and still want it." That sausage might not catch on again—though it's not bad—but a new generation of customers have come to appreciate the old-fashioned way that things are done at Stehlin's.

One more kind of ham that visitors can come across in Greater Cincinnati, especially in Northern Kentucky, is country ham, which comes from a different lineage than the others. It's a Kentucky and southern tradition, born from homesteaders and small farmers who'd smoke their own hams in a smokehouse, curing them so they'd last through a whole year at least. They are salty as can be and are deeply flavored from their long hang, as special in their way as fancy hams from Italy and Spain.

There's still another place where visitors can find a good lineup of the German meats that Cincinnati loves, along with a whole collection of food that weaves together a great deal more of the city's food history.

6

THE PEOPLE'S MARKET

Findlay Market

In 2005, the nonprofit board that runs Findlay Market, the public market that has served shoppers in Over-the-Rhine since 1855, wanted to expand the market's open hours to include Sunday. That would not seem to be a controversial decision; after all, grocery stores are open every day, and it's a common day for the family grocery shopping. But Findlay Market isn't just a grocery store. It's a special place where Cincinnati's food culture—past, present and future—come together as a market and as a history lesson.

Many of the stalls inside the market were run by families who have had businesses there for several generations, whose kids grew up helping them out on the weekend and who still employ only relatives. So, opening on Sundays would be difficult for them. They'd either have to give up a day off or hire non-family members. On the other hand, there were new entrepreneurs in the market without long ties of traditions, and they would benefit from the expanded hours. In the end, it was agreed to try Sunday hours, with all merchants participating—whether eagerly or reluctantly. It has turned out to be a success; Sunday is now the second-busiest day at the market, after Saturday. Another experiment was conducted in 2017 to stay open late on Wednesday nights, but it didn't work out as well, and Findlay still closes around the time most people get off work.

The conflict points out the basic dilemma of Findlay Market in the twenty-first century. Starting as one of the markets that simply existed as a way to sell food to households, it is taking on the characteristics of a tourist attraction and a place to buy specialty products that can't be found anywhere else. In

The plaza at Findlay Market, where shoppers meet and nosh, in 2017. *Courtesy of the* Cincinnati Enquirer *and Liz Dufour.*

its 160 years of existence, the market has served its neighborhood, welcomed immigrants and offered bargains. It has nurtured small businesses and has been a vital community hub, a place where different people mingle, where they run errands but also slow down a little and run into friends and their favorite vendors. The market's past is always an inspiration, but the question is what part of its history can be preserved as the city changes around it.

In the meat shops that line the central market house of this public market, there are remnants of Porkopolis and the old street markets. There are echoes of German immigrant culture in the varieties of sausage and goetta, overlaid with the subsequent history of Over-the-Rhine. Fruit, choices of ribs and turkey necks, gelato, Belgian waffles, cheese and bread are all part of the market. Because the market is old and there are still very traditional ways of doing things in Cincinnati, visitors are always aware of the city's history when they shop. But this is an ever-changing, adaptable place, and shoppers are sure to see new things being introduced. Though when shoppers look closer, new things often turn out to be reimaginings of older ways. This institution hung on through the decades, although it was taken for granted, it was doing things traditionally long enough for its time of relevance to come around again.

Ned Coleman of Camp Washington (*left*) buys potatoes from Allen Lawhorn at Findlay Market in 1987. *Courtesy of the* Cincinnati Enquirer *and Dick Swaim.*

Many other open-air public markets have come and gone since the settling of Cincinnati. Back in the early days of the city, there was a market on Sycamore Street, by the river, where venison and bear meat was sold. By 1852, the decade before the Civil War, there were about six open-air markets in Cincinnati, which, at the time, stretched from the Ohio River to Liberty Pike (now Liberty Street).

James Findlay, a veteran of the War of 1812, a store owner, several-time mayor of Cincinnati and a representative to Congress, is the namesake of the Findlay Market. He and a business partner bought a wooded property with the intention of developing a market. Findlay died in 1835, before the market could be built, but after his wife's death, the couple's executors donated the land to the city for the development of a market named for Findlay. The cornerstone was christened in 1854 with a bottle of Rhine wine broken by five-year-old Marie Hoeffer—at least that's what Marie Hoeffer Lawton told a newspaper reporter in 1929, when she was eighty. Hoeffer also said that wine and newspapers were encased in the foundation stone.

The market was built using cast iron, an unusual and novel choice of building material, and it finally opened in 1855. It was an open-air structure, like a large carport. A subdivision grew up around the market, taking the place of farms. The market's hard-to-knock-down cast iron probably helped it outlive the other markets. But being in the upper part of Over-the-Rhine, an area called the Liberties before it was annexed around the time the market was built, also probably helped. It was out of the path of downtown development, in a practically suburban location. Later in the twentieth century, Over-the-Rhine, especially north of Liberty Street, was neglected. No one wanted to develop anything there, but Findlay held on.

The market also had a very well-organized community of vendors. In 1960, Al Schottelkotte, a columnist at the *Cincinnati Enquirer*, interviewed a vendor at the Sixth Street Market, which was then being closed, who said, "They'd never do it this way to Findlay Market, leave people without a place to go, if the city ever wanted the Findlay Market property. The Findlay Market Association is too tough." The association was, indeed, busy running and promoting the market. For a long stretch of time, the association sponsored Findlay Market Day at Chester Park, then at Coney Island, the amusement park east of town. The festival always included famous sandwiches for a nickel, even long after that was the going price. There were also games and contests there; at the 1914 picnic, there were contests for rolling a peanut uphill with a toothpick, fat men and fat women's races and a giveaway of a full Hungarian wedding. The association also created the Findlay Market Parade in 1919 for baseball's opening day, and Findlay merchants still organize the parade, which begins at the market and proceeds to the ballpark by the river in one of Cincinnati's most enduring and popular traditions.

In the nineteenth century, many political rallies, which often featured torchlight processions, began or ended at the market. The Democrats held their rallies at the Race Street end, and the Republicans held theirs on the Elm Street end. In 1876, General Franz Sigel, a German hero of the Civil War, was the highlight of a Democratic rally that was attended by at least four thousand people who listened to his speech in German. In 1910, Warren G. Harding spoke there during his campaign for governor of Ohio. In the 1940s, the Franciscan friars of nearby St. Francis Seraph sponsored street preaching at the market, with speakers such as Reverend Hyacinth Blocker, who addressed the crowd with "Grace, God's Helping Hand," or Reverend Severin Lamping, who addressed the crowd with "Buy a Share of Heaven Today." Findlay Market wasn't just a market; it was a community center and public gathering place.

But, of course, day in and day out, it was there to sell food. Until the 1930s, only meat could be sold inside the market house. Produce stalls

Inside the market house of Findlay Market, which held only butchers at one time, in 2016. *Courtesy of Carol Highsmith, Library of Congress.*

stretched for blocks along Race Street, and farmers in the surrounding areas hauled in produce from deep in the country or closer truck farms. A farmer named Jimmy Krismer had a three-acre plot on Kirby Road that had cold boxes and greenhouses where he grew everything he sold at the market. The Kunkel family, who were new arrivals from Germany, began selling pickles and sauerkraut the year the market opened, and the family continued "on market" for 150 years. Early on, the whole family pitched in to prepare the cabbage kraut, pickled beans, cabbage, beets and onions (also "pickelilly and pickels," according to a Kunkel business card). A historic photograph in Liz Tilton's book *Cincinnati's Historic Findlay Market* shows a crowd of family members preparing beans as they sit in the alley behind their home at 2112 Vine Street.

Early on, shoppers could buy live chickens at the market. Later, vendors such as Heist butchered chickens on site. Three generations of the Zimmermann family sold poultry they butchered themselves. In 1956, an article by Libby Lackman of the *Enquirer* detailed the process. Ray Zimmermann and one helper would butcher 360 chickens a day, from Tuesday to Thursday, using an automatic dipper for scalding the feathers and an automatic plucker. They sold their whole chickens at Findlay on

Friday and Saturday. His father, said Zimmermann, had to do it "the hard way" and his grandfather "the harder way." Charles Naish sold cookies. He didn't bake them, but he gathered them from local bakeries or from out of state. He sold them in bulk and would assemble a selection for each customer. Rabbit and other wild game was also sold in many stalls. William "Blind" Beck sold fresh eggs. Shoppers could buy pungent fresh-grated horseradish to eat with sausages they had just bought from a man who sat outside the market house. He offered fresh-grated coconut, too. (I wonder what the coconut was for: macaroons? Or possibly coconut cream pie, which the girls in "Wooden Show Hollow" mentioned making, and which became popular around 1900.)

Krismer Bakery sold bread in a stall, with rye and white bread piled deep into a glass-fronted bin. Rose Krismer ran the stall herself for years, after her husband was killed when he fell asleep and his horse stopped on the railroad tracks on his way home. There seemed to be a common phenomenon of stall holders dying young and leaving their widows to run their businesses. In 1942, Mrs. Robert Braun had been running a butcher shop by herself for fifty-four years, ever since her husband had died. It was, at that time, the longest-lasting stall. Italians ran the produce stalls. Rizzo, Catanzaro, Gaudio, Sensio, Caito were all families who sold produce. As the produce business was consolidated, Italians also ran many of the big wholesale houses.

The character of Findlay Market has changed along with the character of the neighborhood. As Italians arrived, they added to the German flavor. Appalachian people who moved up from Kentucky and Tennessee during the 1940s and 1950s had their own ways of shopping, and African Americans were the market's main customers in the 1980s and 1990s. Then, as supermarkets took over the vast majority of grocery shopping trips, Findlay became an object of nostalgia. In 1949, an *Enquirer* article by Jack Raney thought that Findlay Market was "out of the old world" and effused over how all the hawkers "cry their wares" in a charming, old-fashioned way.

In 1957, the *Enquirer*'s book review editor wrote an essay on why he drove from the suburbs to shop at Findlay. He said he was partially "addicted in a mild way to fresh grated coconut." He also liked the feel of the place:

> *You see types of all kinds…and the languages! In one of the shops that specialize in German foods, you can hear a dozen different dialects, including Swabian, Bavarian, Platt-Deutsch, Banatar, Rhineland and second-generation Cincinnati ("Them's good, lady"). In spite of the changes in*

> *population of the quarter from Over-the-Rhine Germans to Over-the-Ohio hill folks, Findlay Market itself not only has managed to survive almost all of the other food markets in town but to retain its character and a lively hustling atmosphere.*

For a long time, some people have felt that Findlay didn't get its due respect. In 1979, Marie Ryckman, the *Enquirer*'s food editor, went on about the market's strawberries and meat—all beautiful and cheap. "Whenever I have visited San Francisco, San Antonio, Chicago or Boston as a food editor, I have been taken to visit a farmer's market each of those cities proudly shows to visitors. That's what we need to do here, too. Show Findlay Market to our visitors and be sure we know it well, too, and its history."

The market was renovated in 1974, but Ryckman was writing this at the beginning of a low point at Findlay Market. When I first arrived in Cincinnati in 1983, it was still fun to shop for the "old world charm," and it was a place

Over-the-Rhine has changed many times since it was built by Germans. In 1985, these residents were looking out of their windows from a building that was first constructed as a German bank. *Courtesy of the* Cincinnati Enquirer *and Ed Reinke.*

for good deals on anything from ribs to filets. If you wanted headcheese or souse, this was the place to look, but the produce in the outside stalls seemed tired. Though I liked the principle of the place, there wasn't much that was fresh and of interest to me.

But it was still an important part of the neighborhood. Over-the-Rhine was occupied, at the time, by the working class and struggling Appalachian people and African Americans. (In 1981, Johnny Cash starred in *The Pride of Jesse Hallam*, a television movie about an illiterate Kentuckian who moved to Cincinnati and worked at a produce store in Findlay Market.) The market offered affordable groceries for the neighborhood and still sold goods personally. People came from around the city for bargains. The city had been running the market, but in 2000, the Corporation for Findlay Market took over management and ran it as a nonprofit business. There was a major remodeling of the market in 2002 and 2003. No one wanted to see Findlay die, even if they never shopped there. It was too important to the city and its past, and it held nostalgic memories for many Cincinnatians.

There had been big changes in Over-the-Rhine. The area went from being a working-class neighborhood to a place of concentrated poverty. Landlords who took federal Section 8 subsidies had been concentrated in the neighborhood; they didn't invest in their properties, and there was no federal money for market-rate development. There was an entrenched conflict for years between advocates for the poor and development interests. Led by activist Buddy Gray, the advocates fought to keep Over-the-Rhine as a place for the poor. They were against anything that might have led to gentrification, including the National Historic District designation of the neighborhood in 1983. They bought buildings so that they wouldn't be developed, but they left them empty as they fought any other kind of investment. Eventually, the whole neighborhood was designated in a city plan as a low-income housing district. In the late 1990s, there was some budding development on Main Street, but it was brought to a halt in March 2001, when Timothy Thomas, a young African American man, was shot and killed by the police. The incident set off public disturbances by people who'd seen enough police shootings. The incident resulted in rioting and the destruction of property, including some stores near Findlay Market.

Activist Buddy Gray was killed by a mentally ill man in 1996, and the battle against gentrification was essentially settled with the formation of 3CDC (Cincinnati Center City Development Corporation) in 2003. Seeing that the city couldn't thrive and that its business community couldn't

George Roth of Roth Produce handing Jan Schaefer of Delhi Township a bag at Findlay Market in Over-the-Rhine. *Courtesy of the* Enquirer *and Kareem Elgazzar.*

recruit talent when a whole swath of buildings to the north of downtown sat empty, business leaders formed 3CDC with millions of dollars available for development. They started by remodeling Fountain Square and then moved to Over-the-Rhine, where they developed the blocks closest to Central Parkway, which they called the Gateway Quarter, around 2007. Washington Park, which fills two blocks north of Thirteenth Street, was redeveloped in 2012, replacing a school, a swimming pool and basketball courts with wading pools, playgrounds, a performance space and a full line-up of activities. Development began moving north. The group 3CDC is seen by some as being too powerful and quasi-governmental without enough public accountability or attention to low-income housing for people who were living in Over-the-Rhine. But it has been extremely successful at what it set out to do.

All of this development brought new, more affluent residents to downtown and Over-the-Rhine, and they became shoppers at Findlay Market. More suburbanites started feeling comfortable going downtown, and they went to Findlay. The market began reinventing itself. Shopping at the market was more fun than going to a supermarket, though it was less efficient. A new culture of foodie-ism brought attention to local traditions, and as the local food movement gained ground, more people wanted to buy their produce from farmers. Shoppers wanted an authentic, urban experience, and they wanted artisanal goods. In other words, they wanted what Findlay Market used to be and what it was still clinging to. Zimmermann's chickens would have gone over very well.

Of course, the city wasn't going to go back to the days when open ceramic bowls held home-pickled tomatoes, but Findlay began to offer what shoppers wanted. The idea of having a true farmers' market back at Findlay was first floated in 1997, though the dedicated farmers' shed didn't open until 2004. Some farmers were concerned that buyers wouldn't pay a little more for local and homegrown produce, but the farmers' market became very popular. It was designed along a rather narrow walkway between the parking lot and the market house that now becomes crowded on the weekends. From bedding plants in the spring through the explosion of tomatoes and corn in the summer and many varieties of apples in the fall, there is a wide choice of fresh bounty in the shed between April and November. Some vendors are organic, like Greenacres Farm in Indian Hill. Some bring other products, like honey and apple cider and baked goods. New kinds of ethnic food stores have started new traditions. Dean's Mediterranean is a tiny store stuffed with gourmet ingredients and Middle Eastern specialties, including house-made yogurt and falafel. The stall was opened by Dean Zaidan in the late 1980s, with roasted nuts as its first product. His daughter Kate has since taken over the store and has brought new energy to the market. Saigon Market has been selling Asian food in a stall on the south side of the market since 1976.

In 1992, Mark and Mike Kroeger took over Kroeger & Sons, the butcher business that their father Paul, an immigrant from Bremen, had opened in 1972. They had played there as children and had helped in the store since they were young teens. After taking over the business, they continued making brats and metts and other wursts, but they also began experimenting with new varieties of sausages. First, they invented a Vidalia onion pork sausage, then a boudin and an andouille, and from there, they went on to develop everything from a Swedish potato to a duck sausage. Their stall became busy, with people waiting several layers deep on a Saturday. They breathed new life into the Cincinnati sausage tradition. But butchering takes a toll, and when Mike and Mark began noticing that they were starting to become arthritic—as their father had—they sold the stall and went to nursing school. Theirs was the first of many businesses that began opening in the market house in the 2010s with a new attitude and offerings.

Dojo Gelato makes Italian ice cream and espresso. Combined in an affogato, the two products have fueled many of my Findlay Market shopping trips. Colonel De Stewart brought spices from all over the world, along with his own special blends, to a small stand at the market that had to expand in size several times. It's a popular stand with chefs and barbecuers. Colonel De Stewart died in 2018, but the stand continues. Madison's, a permanent store on the north side of the market, started with locally grown mushrooms and blackberries from a family farm, and it went on to offer a year-round and daily supply of produce, including produce that was locally grown. Brian Madison, the founder, retired in 2019, but new owners are keeping the tradition. Taste of Belgium, with its fresh waffles, crepes and other European pastries, along with the prepared salads and entrées from Fresh Table, now Gourmand Group, were all for a new, more affluent shopper.

Pho Lang Thang was a Vietnamese café that was started by three Vietnamese-Cincinnatian guys. It had excellent pho and Vietnamese coffee that drew a loyal group to their crowded space full of wonderful smells. The café has since moved across the street. Blue Oven Bakery gets long lines for its artisan bread, which is baked in a wood-fueled oven and ranges from light and airy Italian hubcap or Seedy McSeed to dark rye and loaf breads like Omegatron, which is stuffed with nuts and seeds. For browsers, there are croissants and toasts with toppings. There's also a florist and a wine shop at the market.

Today, more people go to the market to eat and hang out, and fewer go to buy groceries. Vendors found that their revenues from food stamps were beginning to fall off. The market looked very different, especially on the weekends, when it was a lot more crowded. Parking was added—another controversial subject—but the old-time vendors are benefitting from the extra traffic, and they are able to keep up long-standing family traditions. Silverglades still sells a wide variety of cheeses and olives, along with their two choices of chicken salad—one smoked, one with grapes and walnuts. There is still a choice of butchers inside the market house, including Luken's Fish and Bender's Meats. Eckerlin's, which is owned by the Lillis family, the descendants of the original Eckerlins, who had a stall when Findlay Market opened, still makes some of the best goetta in the city (including a very peppery version). Gibb's Meats has been at the market since the 1920s, selling Amish butter, a large selection of cheese and homemade fudge and peanut butter. Butchers like Neil Luken sell high-quality meat. Vendors come and go, but many have been here through good and bad times—through a few generations—and cater to both new and old customers.

In 2016, Findlay Kitchen opened its doors across Elm Street from the market, with a mission of helping small food entrepreneurs get a boost up as they start their business. Some of the small businesses that have started there have moved over to the outdoor lane north of the market, where they sell arepas, Vietnamese food, currywursts, soul food and Filipino pancit. There's now an arepa restaurant next door to a bean-to-bar chocolate store.

Findlay seems to never stay the same, but it always maintains its character. It's the slowing down of shopping, the personal attention across the counter, the appearance of neighbors and friends and the discovery of something new that continues to draw shoppers. It is a must-stop for anyone interested in Cincinnati history. But for most of its history, Findlay was not the only market in town, and its farmers' market is only one of many farmers' markets in Cincinnati today.

7

FROM FARM TO TABLE

In 1985, my husband and I bought our first house in the neighborhood of Pleasant Ridge, and I found that one of the best things about our neighborhood was that, on Mondays, a group of farmers would set up a tailgate market in the parking lot of the neighborhood Catholic church. I'd walk up with the kids in the stroller to buy tomatoes and corn and other fresh produce that had been brought from farms just outside the city. But starting about 2007, my choices for fresh local produce started exploding. Neighborhood markets popped up all over the city. There were weeks in which I'd hit the market in the suburb of Wyoming on Tuesday, in the Northside neighborhood on Thursday and Hyde Park and maybe Findlay Market on the weekend.

By 2012, there were at least forty farmers' markets, most operating once a week and organized by farmers or by neighborhood activists, local food enthusiasts or by a municipality. By then, they were selling a wider variety of goods that often included products like jams, pies and bread. They were open for a longer season, and some even operated in the winter. I was buying more locally grown corn and tomatoes, melons, okra, honey, wood oven–baked bread, Chinese greens, kombucha, mushrooms and flowers than my two-person household could possibly need, but the bounty was irresistible, the products were fresh and vibrant and the idea of helping to create a new, local-food economy was exciting. That's what all the volunteers and farmers at the markets were aiming to do; they wanted people to eat local, support local farmers, cut down on food miles and improve the quality of their nutrition. It all felt new, though of course, it was one more way in which food innovation was reworking the past. Eating local wasn't new, though it had been abandoned for a while.

> *Cincinnati is well fed. She eats a full, hearty meal and takes pleasure in the reflection that none can find better food to devour than herself. Her board creaks under the choicest extracts ever lavished upon humanity by the fertile soil of a happy valley.*

That's from a story appeared in the *Cincinnati Enquirer* on August 5, 1894. It describes, in great detail, a vendor's day at the Sixth Street Market back when the city ate locally without calling it that.

> *Its little band of merrymakers outside of* [Cincinnati's] *corporation line have engaged themselves to journey three times a week into her midst, pitch their tents, strike camp, and besides doing a thrifty business make merry until the mart is closed. This army consists of market people, and a jollier, hardier band of troops never campaigned in any country....*
>
> *If you want to see women of brawn and sinew, go early to the Sixth Street Market and watch them unload their wagons. Here you find them twirling barrels of potatoes, cabbage, apples,* [et cetera], *with strength that is GOOD TO SEE.*

The Sixth Street Market lined the street from Vine to Mound Streets and all along many of the streets that crossed it. The vendors at this market would arrive from Kentucky, Indiana and Ohio farms the night before, sleep in their wagons and set up their stalls. Besides the farmers selling produce, there was a man who ground horseradish and another named Caesar Cruianco, from Bologna, Italy, who sold watermelons and bananas. From the back of their wagons, they sold wholesale "to the big hotels, to boarding house women, jobbers, peddlers and small dealers," according to the same newspaper article. On the other side, facing the street, they sold retail. Forty-nine years later, *The WPA Guide* described the market as a tourist attraction: "The makeshift kiosks lining both sides of the street, with their pyramids of melons, beans, berries, tomatoes and other fruits and vegetables, the fast patter of vendors, and the snooping and haggling of shoppers, make a colorful place."

The Sixth Street Market was one of several markets that did business in Cincinnati between the time of the city's founding and today. Early on, there

The Sixth Street Market in an undated photo. Commission houses, or wholesalers, line the block behind the area where the farmers set up. *Courtesy of the* Cincinnati Enquirer.

was an Upper and Lower Market, where men sold bear and venison. There were vegetables for sale there, along with paw paws, wild grapes, hickory nuts and chestnuts. The Fifth Street Market opened in 1829, and the Canal Market opened in 1829. There were nine markets in the downtown basin of Cincinnati over the years: Fifth Street, Wade Street, Canal, Court Street, Jabez Elliott Flower Market, Sixth Street, Pearl Street, a farmers' wholesale market and Findlay.

In 1895, Sixth Street Market got a new butchers' market house. It was designed by Cincinnati's most famous architect, Samuel Hannaford, and looked more like a castle than a place to buy pork chops. Inside, there were sixty-four meat, poultry and dairy stands. Outside, there were over a hundred stands set up on market days. This was where the farmers of the land surrounding Cincinnati met customers face to face and sold them a wide variety of what was grown in the fertile soils of the Ohio Valley. In the second half of the nineteenth century, Ohio farmers provided virtually all of the food consumed in Ohio and exported more. Farmers near cities did well, making land near Cincinnati worth $100 an acre, twice the average for the state. Most farms were diversified, which allowed them to survive poor market conditions for particular crops and made their farms mostly self-sufficient. The farms' animals provided fertilizer. Farmers could take their corn and wheat to a local gristmill. In Hamilton County, there were once thirty-four water-powered gristmills in operation.

Charlotte Pieper's novel *Wooden Shoe Hollow* illustrates the life of one local farming community. The German farmers of Wooden Shoe Hollow near Spring Grove Cemetery (who did, in fact, wear wooden shoes) grew crops like celery, lima beans, cucumbers, tomatoes, butter beans and radishes on their rich bottomland, and their soil was enriched with manure from nearby horse stables. They brought their goods to the Cincinnati markets, where they sold to either consumers or wholesalers. Around 1912, when the novel is set, greenhouses began to come into use. They were controversial at first, but they caught on, and for a time, they were a thriving business in the area. Greenhouses were mostly used to raise tomatoes well past their usual season. When I moved to Cincinnati in 1983, I had friends who lived near Spring Grove Cemetery, next to a big greenhouse full of tomatoes, but in the years since then, the tomatoes have disappeared. Some greenhouses remain in the original families' hands, but they now grow flowers and bedding plants.

The meeting between farmer and shopper began to change in the early twentieth century. The central part of Cincinnati became polluted, disease-prone and crowded, so those who could afford to moved to the hilltop neighborhoods, where there were no public markets. The markets did not keep up with changing standards of sanitation. An 1894 article about the Sixth Street Market noted that the meat market "is literally alive with rats. There must be at least 15,000 rats in, under and about this place." In 1913, the markets were described as "ridiculous, old-fashioned and unsanitary public markets, where food was sold on rotted dirty old-fashioned cobblestone streets. Animals are driven through the streets to slaughterhouses." (This was years after Fanny Trollope made the same complaint.)

New, more convenient ways of shopping became available. Bernard Heinrich Kroger, who changed his name to Barney Henry or B.H. Kroger, was a pioneer and innovator when it came to more convenient grocery stores and, eventually, supermarkets. The son of German immigrants to Cincinnati who lost their dry goods store in the panic of 1873, Kroger entered the grocery business with a partner, and they opened their first store, which faced the Pearl Street Market, in 1883. A flood and an accident that killed their delivery wagon horse almost wiped them out in their first

Flying pigs atop the steam stacks on a sculpture in Bicentennial Park represent "the angelic spirits of all the pigs that were slaughtered and were building blocks of Cincinnati's prosperity." *Courtesy of Raúl Arias.*

"Pork Packing in Cincinnati," by Henry Farny, shows the disassembly line that was invented in Cincinnati. *Courtesy of the Library of Congress.*

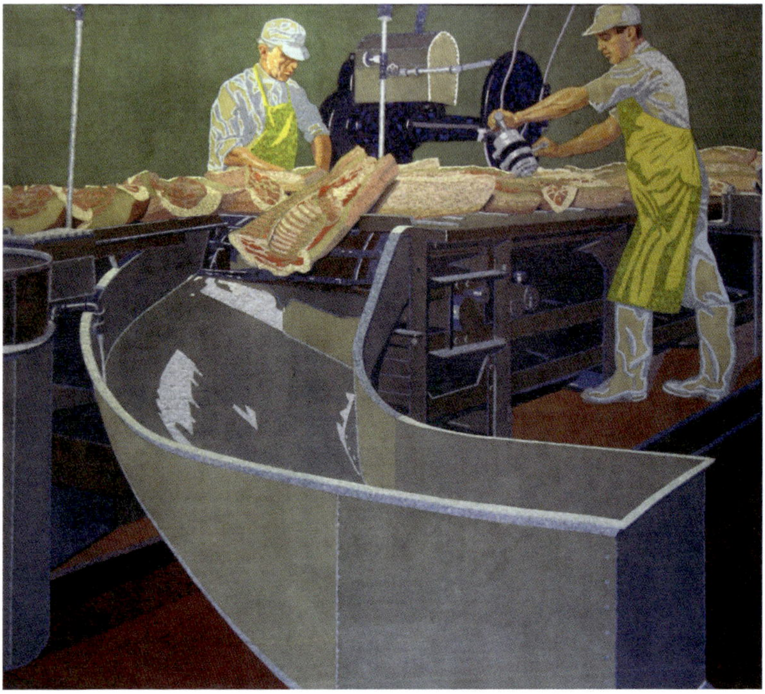

In 1933, artist Winold Reiss created mosaic murals of the workers of Cincinnati for the rotunda of Union Terminal. This mural portrays butchers at E. Kahn's & Sons. *Courtesy of the* Cincinnati Enquirer *and Glenn Hartong.*

Bill Dorl (*left*) and Steve Blank (*right*) hanging freshly made mettwurst in preparation for smoking at Stehlin's Meat Market in Colerain Township in 2013. *Courtesy of the* Cincinnati Enquirer *and Gary Landers.*

Above: John Keating from Mariemont (*right*) and Akhil Rachamadugu from downtown (*left*) race beer barrels during the Gemuetlichkeit Games to kick off Oktoberfest in Cincinnati. *Courtesy of the* Cincinnati Enquirer *and Leigh Taylor.*

Left: Mettwursts made by the men of Fleming Road United Church of Christ being smoked over donated applewood for the church's annual mett dinner. *Courtesy of the* Cincinnati Enquirer *and Polly Campbell.*

Above: Findlay Market in Over-the-Rhine, which has been in operation since 1855, is still a market and a community center. *Courtesy of the* Cincinnati Enquirer *and Liz Dufour.*

Left: An advertisement for Fleischmann's Yeast, which was originally made in Cincinnati. The advertisement features Germans eating cake and coffee in the afternoon. *Courtesy of the* Cincinnati Enquirer.

Greg Gottenbusch, the owner of Servatii Pastry Shop & Deli, taking a strawberry coffeecake out of the display case in 2017. *Courtesy of the* Cincinnati Enquirer *and Meg Vogel.*

Shannon Tumey serves chili at Camp Washington Chili in 2015. *Courtesy of the* Cincinnati Enquirer *and Liz Dufour.*

Pleasant Ridge Chili at dusk. It's open until 4:30 a.m. every day except for Sunday. *Courtesy of Neil Sharrow.*

A nectar soda being made at Graeter's. *Courtesy of Raúl Arias.*

Chocolate hardens inside a funnel-shaped hole in a pot of Graeter's vanilla ice cream. This is how Graeter's makes its famous chocolate chips. *Courtesy of the* Cincinnati Enquirer *and Michael E. Keating.*

A United Dairy Farmers banana split. *Courtesy of the* Cincinnati Enquirer *and Meg Vogel.*

Left: A mosaic mural outside the Moerlein taproom in Over-the-Rhine honors the servers of Cincinnati's old beer halls. *Courtesy of Raúl Arias.*

Below: Sausage queen Luis Balladares at Bockfest in 2019. Balladeres won the title after a friend secretly added his name to the list of contestants. *Courtesy of the* Cincinnati Enquirer *and Ryan Terhune.*

A promotional lithograph for Woodside Co.'s "Laugh At" cigars illustrates the scene on Vine Street in its heyday, including its brass rail for drinking, cigars, beer and racy art. *Courtesy of the Library of Congress.*

A modern version of the beer hall: Rhinegeist's taproom in the former Moerlein Brewery in Over-the-Rhine. *Courtesy of Raúl Arias.*

A gorgonzola piccante pizza coming out of the wood-burning oven at A Tavola, a pizza restaurant on Vine Street in Over-the-Rhine. *Courtesy of the* Cincinnati Enquirer *and David Sorcher.*

Taste of Belgium's waffles have become an iconic food of Cincinnati. This photograph was taken in 2015. *Courtesy of the* Cincinnati Enquirer *and Madison Schmidt.*

Wielert's Saloon, one of the many beer halls that populated Over-the-Rhine in the late 1800s. *Sketch by Henry Farny, courtesy of the Public Library of Cincinnati and Hamilton County.*

Ravioli ready to go through the window at the Sacred Heart Ravioli Festival at Sacred Heart Church in Camp Washington in 2019. *Courtesy of Raúl Arias.*

Scotti's Italian restaurant, with its free-form tiling job and classic pasta, veal, beef and chicken dishes, is one of the oldest and most distinctive restaurants in Cincinnati. *Courtesy of the* Cincinnati Enquirer *and Carrie Cochran.*

A smiley face cookie from Busken. *Courtesy of Busken.*

The bathtub outside Arnold's Bar and Grill, which is equipped with a lawnmower motor for parades, is a twin to the famous gin bathtub inside the restaurant. *Courtesy of Raúl Arias.*

Mark and Sara Frommeyer, the owners of Blue Oven Bread, selling their naturally fermented bread, which is baked in a wood-fired oven at the Hyde Park Farmers' Market, where lines of customers often form. *Courtesy of Neil Sharrow.*

Left: Big steaks cooked at a high temperature with a steak rub crust are what draw people to Jeff Ruby's Steakhouse. *Courtesy of the* Cincinnati Enquirer *and Jeff Swinger.*

Below: Listermann Brewing Company created a canned beer with artwork that honors the artists of King Records, an important record label from Cincinnati. *Courtesy of the Listermann Brewing Company.*

Right: Bouquet Restaurant has been one of the strongest supporters of using local products. Their duck with blackberries, kohlrabi, dragon beans and purslane. *Courtesy of the* Cincinnati Enquirer *and Meg Vogel.*

Below: A five-way at Camp Washington Chili. It's made from spaghetti, chili, beans, onions and cheese. *Courtesy of the* Cincinnati Enquirer *and Meg Vogel.*

A beer from Taft's Brewing Company, which is housed in a church that was built in the 1850s in Over-the-Rhine. It was named for President William Howard Taft, a Cincinnati native. *Courtesy of the* Cincinnati Enquirer *and Cara Owsley.*

Senate Pub got things rolling on Vine Street in Over-the-Rhine with hot dogs with fancy toppings. *Top to bottom*: a trailer dog, a croque madame and a Chicago. *Courtesy of the* Cincinnati Enquirer *and Amanda Rossmann.*

The first Kroger store, built in 1883 at 66 Pearl Street, sold brooms, pyramids of cans and cigars. *Courtesy of the* Cincinnati Enquirer.

year, but Kroger bought out his partner and proceeded to make a wild success of his business.

Kroger believed in high-quality groceries, plenty of advertising and selling cheaper than everyone else. In the beginning, customers came to the store, ordered what they wanted and had it delivered to them by wagon. In Kroger's case, the wagons, which were painted red and gold and looked like the circus, doubled as advertising. He took out advertisements in the daily newspapers, sometimes buying whole pages. He started his own in-store bakery and butcher, and he sold his mother's sauerkraut and pickles, both to cut his own costs and to make shopping more convenient. His second store was opened in 1884, and by 1902, he had forty locations. Around 1916, he introduced self-service so that shoppers could choose their own groceries and take them home themselves. He also did not believe in extending credit to regular customers, as old-fashioned grocers did. These words of wisdom appeared in the *Cincinnati Cookbook*, which was published in 1908: "There is no way in which you can save as much as by buying your groceries and meat at one of the Kroger Grocery & Baking Co.'s stores where you have to pay cash. This takes away the temptation of buying more things than you can afford.—BH Kroger"

On the other side of the farm-consumer equation, farming changed dramatically in the nineteenth century. In 1835, Obed Hussey of Hamilton County, just north of Cincinnati, invented a mechanized reaper, a horse-drawn contraption that revolutionized harvesting. Though Hussey's invention came first, Cyrus McCormick also devised a somewhat different reaper, which outperformed and outsold Hussey's. Thus began the mechanization of farms, which gave them the ability to produce more output with fewer people—though it made farming more expensive. Gradually, farms became bigger and more specialized. After World War II, the change on farms was radical. Chemical fertilizer and herbicides made farming more productive and required less labor. In Ohio, agribusiness concentrated on corn, soybeans and dairy. Other parts of the country became more efficient at growing particular crops, like wheat and apples.

In 1945, there were 221,000 farms in Ohio. By 1995, there were only 74,000, and only 3 percent of Ohioans lived in full-time farm families; most farmers only farmed part time. With better transportation and refrigeration, distribution became centralized and super-sized. Kroger Co. was a major pioneer in this trend. Barney Kroger basically invented the low margin in the grocery business. He bought produce wholesale by the railcar load and kept prices as low as possible, relying on volume for profit. He cut out middlemen by buying his own ingredients and manufacturing his own products. In 1901, he engaged in a bread pricing war, dropping the price of his loaves from the standard six cents to three cents, enraging other bakers. His innovations and drive made him rich. Just months before the stock market crash of 1929, Kroger sold his stocks in the company for $28 million. By the 2000s, Kroger was the largest grocery chain in the country. It has its headquarters on Central Parkway in downtown Cincinnati.

Local, smaller-scale farmers found it hard to penetrate this large supermarket system. Produce was shipped long distances so that the taste and quality suffered. But some markets hung on as an alternative for buying and selling vegetables. The Sixth Street Market operated until 1960, when it was torn down to make way for an on-ramp to I-75.

Another market, where local farmers sold wholesale with larger volume and cheaper prices, was forced to move from the spot where it was open all day, every day, when the city wanted its land for a parking lot. It eventually moved to the east end of town, by Lunken Airport. The market still operates as a farmers' market daily, though it's not wholesale, and it's only a remnant of the market that once had a thousand farmers. So, for a long time, if Cincinnatians wanted a fresh flavorful tomato, they had to grow it themselves or take a trip to the Lunken Market or out to a farm in the

The last day of the Sixth Street Market, December 31, 1959, just before it was torn down for a highway on-ramp. *Courtesy of the* Cincinnati Enquirer *and Ran Cochran.*

country. When I first moved to Cincinnati in the 1980s, there was a market store on Roundbottom Road that sold some local produce. It was the first time I had ever truly had fresh broccoli, and it was a revelation. There were orchards for locally grown fruit and cider, and some farms opened their berry fields for pick-your-own, but locally grown food was a tiny niche.

Then, in the early 2000s, based on the idea that industrial scale and techniques might not be suitable for the production of food, a new local food movement was started around the country. Michael Pollan's book *The Omnivore's Dilemma* pointed out the problems with a food system built around subsidizing corn used for animal feed, sweetener and processed foods. People became aware of the distorting effect of crop subsidies, the horrors of large-scale feeding operations and the environmental impact of shipping food for thousands of miles. "Locavore" was the word of the year in 2007. It was a movement based on a regard for how things had been done in the past; it was based around trying to reestablish certain structures that had been eroded over the last one hundred years or so.

Cincinnati began building its own local food movement, re-creating the farmer-eater relationship of those early markets and exploring sustainable growing. There were two established organic farms that served as teaching and training centers near Cincinnati: Turner Farm and Greenacres. Both were in Indian Hill, a wealthy suburb of Cincinnati, and experimenting and teaching was central to both of their missions. Many farmers in Kentucky were incentivized to switch from growing tobacco to growing specialty crops, or grass-fed beef, with a subsidy from the state's settlement payment in the tobacco suit of 1998. Restaurants were among the first customers of local produce. Sallie Ransohoff started by growing basil on rented land in Wooden Shoe Hollow; she later added tomatoes and other produce and sold exclusively and personally to chefs like Jean-Robert de Cavel. They bought from her because her produce was high-quality, and she grew to their specifications.

Findlay Market opened its farmers' shed in 2004; then markets started springing up in neighborhoods. Two of the earliest, and still most significant, of these markets were in Wyoming and Hyde Park. Both had active market managers who made visits to farms to make sure they were truly growing their own produce with sustainable farming methods. By 2015, there were about fifty farmers' markets in the Greater Cincinnati area. Every year, it seemed, markets opened earlier in the season and closed later. Some even established winter markets. Farmers diversified what they grew and brought to market. Though corn and tomatoes are always popular, shoppers can now find colorful varieties of heirloom tomatoes, herbs, kale and other greens, okra, Israeli melons, cauliflower, black walnuts, bunches of roses, mushrooms, dried beans, corn, asparagus, varieties of garlic, cipollini onions and broccoli.

Shoppers will also see "Indiana melons" for sale, a name for cantaloupes that is left over from a time when certain counties in Indiana grew the best-tasting melons. It has become less common to come across local "mangoes," once a common way of referring to green peppers. The peppers earned that name because actual mangoes came to market as exotic fruits in pickled, preserved form. The name mango then evolved to mean anything pickled, like peppers. The word mango then came to just mean pepper, even if it wasn't pickled. The produce in Kentucky markets has its own characteristics. Shoppers can find heirloom varieties of shucking beans and many kinds of pole beans or half-runners to cook slowly with a piece of ham. If they're lucky, shoppers might even find a jar of homemade sorghum.

Farmers' markets have also been a place for food artisans to get a start. It's a low-cost, low-commitment way to try out a food product that might

Erma Griffith of Cold Spring, Kentucky, selling her Erma's Sweets jams, jellies and honey. *Courtesy of the* Community Recorder *and Nancy Daly.*

have commercial potential. I have written many of my favorite stories about people who are passionately working on growing, making and selling food products. I have checked sap lines with Dan Berger on his farm in Warren County, and I have sat in the sweet steam of the maple syrup evaporation house. I've seen the church kitchen where Jordan Aversman and Jennifer De Marco first started making their raw pickled vegetables as Fab Ferments, and I have visited them years later at their kombucha bar. I've seen Sara and Mark Frommeyer of Blue Oven Bread bake bread in a wood-fired oven on their farm, matching each bread's baking requirements to the temperature of the oven as it cools from blazing hot to regular hot. The baker starts with light loaves that cook quickly when the fire is high and ends with whole-grain, dense breads that cook in a less-blazing temperature. I've seen cows step up to a milking machine to give milk that turns into Ed-Mar cheese, and I have tasted complex aged cheeses made by Eduardo Rodriguez of My Artisano Cheese. I've spent time with eighty-five-year-old Ed Motz as he was gathering and cracking black walnuts, and I've chased turkeys at Greenacres Farm. I've seen how Walnut Ridge Acres extends its season with hoop houses, and I've wandered through orchards and seen apples crushed to cider. I've been to Grassland Graze's fields of cattle grazing 100 percent on grass, and I have visited people who are trying to farm like those early Ohio farmers did, growing a diversity of crops along with raising pigs, cattle and chickens, trying to find ways to sell their products for enough money to sustain their work.

Carriage House Farms in North Bend is one of those small, diversified operations. Its owner, Richard Stewart, is out in front on innovations in local food. The farm has been in his family since 1844, but for much of that time it has been rented out for growing corn and soybeans. Some of the land is occupied by a riding stable. But Stewart began planting vegetables there around 2000. Now, the farm supplies chefs and consumers with unusual and high-quality produce, including fresh ginger, Asian pears, all kinds of radishes and greens. The farm has a five-hundred-member CSA (Community Supported Agriculture), an arrangement in which consumers pay ahead for a regular delivery of produce, thus giving farmers some predictable income.

The farm has sold honey since the beginning, along with foraged elderberry and spicebush berries. It added grains, which it sells whole and ground. Stewart, who was a graphic designer before he was a farmer, wants to use the farm as an education center, where people can come together to learn. Some of the city's best chefs have cooked on a little terrace on the side of a hill overlooking the gardens. Now, Stewart is making an interesting line of MadHouse vinegar using unsuccessful batches of beer from MadTree brewery, mislabeled wine that can't be sold, batches of coffee, corn and any food that's surplus and can be fermented and distilled.

Some parlayed their exposure in the markets into much bigger operations. I'll never forget my first taste of Jean-Francois Flechet's Liège-style waffles at the Hyde Park Market. It was a rich, pastry-like waffle, and it was like nothing I'd had before. Flechet was an emigrant from Belgium who'd gotten an advanced economics degree before becoming involved in inventing a hot food vending machine. While that project was stalled, he started making the waffles from his homeland to bring in some money. For a while, it seemed that anywhere a few people were gathered, whether they were at a street fest or the farmers' market, a Belgian waffle cart was there. After moving between several unlucky locations, Taste of Belgium opened on Vine Street. It now has four full-fledged cafés and a stand in Findlay Market. Flechet even had a stand at the Reds' Great American Ball Park for a few seasons. Fireside Pizza started bringing its wood-burning oven

Megan Groves (*left*), Renee Koerner (*middle*) and Keith Koerner (*right*) remove a paddlefish before they harvest its eggs for caviar at Big Fish Farms in Bethel in 2017. *Courtesy of the* Cincinnati Enquirer *and Cara Owsley.*

to the Wyoming Market and later went on to open a restaurant in Walnut Hills in Cincinnati's oldest surviving firehouse.

One of the most remarkable local food stories I've covered is Big Fish Farms. After a long career in high-end dining, Renee Koerner decided to begin ranching paddlefish for caviar. Paddlefish, prehistoric fish with no scales, are native to the Ohio River and have been fished for their eggs, which make a fairly high-quality substitute for sturgeon caviar. Koerner raises them in local lakes and large ponds, where they swim continuously near the bottom, feeding on zooplankton and avoiding most conventional fishing methods. It takes the fish about ten years to reach maturity and for the females to produce roe. Koerner then retrieves fish in the middle of winter, while their eggs are still firm, harvests as much as two to three pounds of roe from each female by slitting open their belly and carefully salts and tins it. It is delicious—comparable to osetra caviar. The flesh of the fish is very different from other fish; it's firm, solid and mild meat, almost like chicken breast, and some restaurants serve it in the winter.

Restaurants have been a crucial part of Cincinnati's local food scene. With their dedication to high-quality products, they are often the first customer for farms that are getting into growing produce. Restaurants have also introduced consumers to the farmers who grew their tomatoes, lamb or honey. Chefs like Julie Francis, who opened Aioli and Nectar, bought goods from farmers, put their names on the menu and often hosted events that featured them. Stephen Williams at Bouquet in Covington spent years building up his relationships with farmers, butchers and other suppliers. Nino Loreto of Panino regularly used to have whole pigs delivered to his kitchen, where he butchered the meat and made charcuterie cured in his own aging room in the restaurant. Chris Burns concentrates on the bounty and traditions of Kentucky at his Commonwealth Bistro in Covington. In Mason, Todd Hudson's Wildflour has a network of local suppliers.

It's not easy for busy chefs to deal with farmers directly and vice versa, so often, chefs don't coordinate with a wide variety of farms. And farmers would rather spend time in the field than driving to restaurants. In 2014, Alice Chalmers, a believer in the importance of a strong local food economy, started a business called Ohio Valley Food Connection. Her idea was to create a mechanism between supply and demand. Farmers could post on her website what they have available, chefs order what they want and she would deliver it. Some of her farmers have been able to drop

Alice Chalmers, the owner of Ohio Valley Food Connection, picking up vegetables at the Madeira Winter Farm Market to deliver to restaurant chefs in 2015. *Courtesy of the* Cincinnati Enquirer *and Cara Owsley.*

a farmers' market or two and devote more time to farming, and chefs have been able to buy much more local produce in a season. OVFC has expanded to serve households as well as restaurants, and it has increased its range toward Louisville and Dayton.

Food incubators have helped small food producers get started in making artisanal products. Rachel DesRochers, who started Grateful Grahams graham cracker bakery, has opened two food incubators to give new food entrepreneurs their first kitchen space as they test their products. Findlay Market has gotten into helping new entrepreneurs with Findlay Kitchen, and Mortar has coached minority entrepreneurs.

So, in Cincinnati it would be quite possible for a dedicated shopper with canning skills and a deep freeze to make local foods a year-round significant part of their diet. Others, however, can enjoy it during the growing season. Local producers have made progress in making it easier for them and consumers to find each other. Even Kroger has gotten on the local food train, truly making it easier for local food producers to get their products on the shelves and brand their produce in-store with local food markets.

Local food artisans who are getting their start in a public market isn't new. It's how one of our most beloved brands got its start.

8

ICE CREAM AND THE STUBBORN GRAETERS

In June 2002, just as the ice cream season was starting, Oprah Winfrey ate some Graeter's ice cream on her show, looked a few million people in the eye and said, "This is the best ice cream I've ever had." You can imagine what happened next. The family ice cream company that had previously concentrated on selling ice cream by the scoop in Cincinnati was deluged with mail orders. That month, they shipped six thousand pints packed in dry ice over a time period in which they would usually ship about sixty. You could, after that, think of Graeter's history as pre-Oprah and post-Oprah. Before, it was a Cincinnati secret, and after, it was a brand that was competing nationally. Both eras are centered on a Cincinnati company sticking to its values.

The word *stubborn* has come up a lot when I've written stories about traditional Cincinnati food businesses. It usually means, "We know it's hard, the way we do things. We don't care. That's how we're going to keep doing it." Bob Graeter, the president of Graeter's Ice Cream, has used that very word about the company that was founded by his great-grandfather and has been run by his family since 1870. I haven't heard the current members of the Aglamesis family use the word *stubborn* about their ice cream company, Aglamesis Brothers, but the fact that their ice cream and candy shop has been in the same location, selling the same things since 1908 suggests it has a commitment to doing things the way it's always done them.

A scoop of butter pecan in a waffle cone at Graeter's. *Courtesy of Graeter's.*

The Aglamesis brothers were Greek, as many candy store owners at the time were. The Graeters were German. Stubbornness can't be ethnically ascribed to Cincinnati's two oldest ice cream operations. But to both, stubbornness means that they haven't messed around with their original formulas, and they haven't adapted to what everyone else is doing, like whipping a lot of air into their ice creams, going low-fat or adding frozen yogurt. In 1988, when Dick Graeter was asked by a reporter whether Graeter's would be making frozen yogurt, which was quite popular then, he replied, "Absolutely not. We'll just wait until the fad passes." In 2010, Graeter's opened a new modern plant. In recent years, it has opened retail shops in new cities and expanded its shipping operations, but it hasn't modernized its "French pot" process, and it's kept the butterfat at 17 percent.

The first Graeter, a barber, came to the United States from Germany and settled in Madison, Indiana. He was apparently a strict, even cruel, father, and his son Louis Charles left home as a teenager to get away from him. Louis went to Cincinnati, and in 1868, just three years after the end of the Civil War, he was making ice cream by hand in one of the public markets. He made the ice cream by stirring it in a pail set in a bucket of salted ice. He grew his business, hired people to help, got married and seemed to be on his way. In 1883, he had two wagons to deliver the fresh ice cream. While it's possible that Louis had the family quality of stubbornness, he wasn't too steady. He left his wife and the business to take off for California, where he got married again. (His photographs do show him to have been a good-looking man.) But he eventually shed himself of that wife as well and came back to Cincinnati around the turn of the century. Once he was back in Cincinnati, he was able to step back into the business with his brother, who had been tending it while he was off in California.

Feckless as he may have been, he did something very smart. In 1900, he married Regina Berger, the daughter of a successful businessman, who was twenty years his junior. They lived above the ice cream shop in Walnut Hills. Regina had a good head for business, which was proven after 1919, when Louis was killed by a streetcar. Regina was forty-four years old, and she stepped into his shoes and took charge in a way that not many women of the time would have thought themselves capable of doing. She ran the shop for thirty-six years, and she not only maintained the business, she grew it. She built six more stores and renovated a building on Reading Road into a production facility. She also added a candy and bakery business. She was at the head of Graeter's through World War I, the Great Depression and World War II, and she didn't retire until 1955.

During her time, Graeter's began making its ice cream in cypress wood pots. The ice cream mixture, including eggs, sugar and cream, was spun from the middle and froze against the sides. Men would then take large paddles and scrape the frozen ice cream from the sides. This was done 2.5 gallons at a time. This is, more or less, how everyone made ice cream—in batches. Continuous freezer technology, which was easier and cheaper, came along in the 1950s. Then, shops didn't have to make 2.5 gallons in one batch, scrape it out and start over; they could just pour the ingredients in one end and keep turning it into ice cream. By the 1950s, this was the primary way ice cream was made. Very good ice cream can be made this way, but it also offers the opportunity to add air to the mix, making the product lighter and cheaper. This made ice cream more affordable, but it was not as rich, dense or creamy on the tongue. And with freezers at home and big freezers in grocery stores, more people ate ice cream at home instead of going to a parlor for a treat.

Those in charge of the shop at the time, Regina's sons, were too cheap—or too stubborn—and their business was too small to become a player in the field of moderately good, inexpensive grocery store ice cream. So, Graeter's kept making its old-fashioned stuff and selling it in Cincinnati by the scoop

Workers at Graeter's making ice cream with the cedar French pots in 1981. *Courtesy of the* Cincinnati Enquirer *and Allan Kain.*

to customers who loved it. They made a living, they worked very hard and they were proud of their product. Wilmer Graeter invented one of Graeter's signatures: the big, soft chocolate chips. These are made by pouring melted chocolate into the ice cream as it freezes, creating the chips that get people hooked on Graeter's. They are not the hard, brittle or tiny chips that many chocolate chip flavors contain; these chips range in size from a flake to a finger's worth of dark chocolate. One of the great pleasures of eating a cone of black raspberry chip is when your tongue discovers a particularly rich lode of chocolate, which sometimes stretches down to the bottom of the cone. Even though it's frozen in ice cream, its texture is soft and melts on contact with your tongue.

It seems that the United States, starting in the 1960s, settled into a long period of food mediocrity, when efficiency and technology took over everything from farming corn to fast food and orange juice. (Remember Tang?) The widespread motto regarding old ways of doing things seemed to be "Why bother when the future is here, and it's cheaper, faster and good enough?" This was not Graeter's motto. Though the shop sometimes made more money with its bakery goods than its ice cream, it kept it up. When high milkfat was regarded as a frozen heart attack, it kept it up.

So, in the 1980s, when Häagen-Dazs introduced its high-fat ice cream and Ben and Jerry's invented flavors that were chock-full of extra add-ins, when foodies started using words like super premium and "low overrun," stubbornness kept Graeter's there to be discovered. Now, Graeter's wasn't just a favorite among people who were proud of their hometown; it was gourmet and a favorite of foodies. People loved discovering it in—of all places—Cincinnati. And, by the way, it bore the name of an actual family, not a random assortment of letters and umlauts made to seem Scandinavian, like Häagen-Dazs. It has a genuine heritage behind it.

The shop's current owners, Regina's great-grandsons, Bob, Dick and Chip Graeter, have taken the company a huge step forward based on this authenticity. They built a new plant and invested in new branding and distribution. The main area of growth has been selling pints through Kroger. But at their plant on Regina Graeter Way in Bond Hill, where the company has thirty-six batch freezers—thirty-two more than the previous plant—I have seen men with long paddles, pushing the frozen ice cream down into the freezers, and chocolate being poured into the top to freeze into those signature jackpot chips.

I like to take visitors to the Museum Center in the former Union Terminal building, west of downtown, for a Graeter's cone. There is a delightful little café off the huge imposing rotunda with its murals of Cincinnati history and industry. Once a tearoom, then a lounge for the USO, it is completely covered in spring-green tiles and decorated with flowers. They're all from Rookwood, the great art pottery company that made tiles and pottery in Mount Adams (founded and run by Maria Longworth, the granddaughter of winemaker Nicholas Longworth). Graeter's serves a limited menu of its ice creams there.

Graeter's has been around for 160 years or so. Aglamesis Brothers is somewhat younger, at 110 years. But while Graeter's stores are modern, the Aglamesis Ice Cream Parlor in Oakley has the look and experience of a different era. This parlor has been in its current spot for a long time. It used to buy its milk and cream from a dairy farm across the street. The shop's Charlie Chaplin candy was first sold when its namesake was in a new movie that was showing at a nearby theater. The interior of the shop maintains its marble counter and Tiffany-style lamps. If you sit at one of the café tables by the front windows, someone will come to take your order. And the ice cream is batch-made behind the store.

Thomas and Nicholas Aglamesis, immigrants from Greece, opened a confectionary in Norwood (a small city that is surrounded by Cincinnati)

Graeter's mint chocolate chip ice cream being made in Graeter's new facility with the same 2.5-gallon pots in 2015. *Courtesy of the* Cincinnati Enquirer *and Madison Schmidt.*

The interior of the Aglamesis ice cream and candy store around 1914 or 1915. *Courtesy of Aglamesis.*

in 1908. It was one of many Greek-owned sweetshops and chocolatiers in the city, long before Snickers bars and Reese's Cups were available at cash registers everywhere. The brothers moved to Oakley in 1913, but they didn't open their second location in Montgomery until sixty-seven years later. On the shop's one hundredth birthday, I asked *Enquirer* readers to send me their memories of Aglamesis, and many people's replies showed the emotional connection that can be made when an establishment sells something delicious. People often went to the shop for special occasions, like dates and excursions with grandparents. One reader said her parents were eating ice cream there when the Japanese attacked Pearl Harbor; another remembered picking out a nickel's worth of candy before a movie.

The business has always remained in the family. Jim Aglamesis presided there for many years after coming home from Korea. Now, his daughter Dianne Lytle and son Randy Young run things. They follow their father's example. "We survived because Dad was diligent, considerate of customers and always believed in being good to people, not cheapening his product," Lytle told me. The candy counter at Aglamesis, which runs along one side of the narrow shop, accented everywhere in pink, is as enticing as the ice cream side. Some of the chocolates are still hand-dipped, as they all used to be. Candy-dipping was a skilled job that employed mostly women.

Cincinnati is also home to the United Dairy Farmers (UDF) chain of convenience stores. This chain was started by Carl Lindner Sr. and his three sons and daughter in Norwood. At the time, milk and other dairy products were delivered by milkmen. The Lindners figured they could offer much cheaper products by stocking them at a convenient store. (Seventy-five years later, the old delivery method is in style again.) Originally, customers could bring their own bowls to the store and get a sundae. Eventually, the store created something it called a "walking sundae," which customers could take away. One of the Lindner sons, Carl Jr., parlayed UDF's success into many other businesses, including a bank, a chain of grocery stores, United Fruit and an insurance company. He eventually became one of the richest men in the United States. His brother Robert took charge of UDF. Like any convenience store, UDF sells cigarettes, beer, a lot of snacks and basic groceries, as well as gas. But every store also has what it calls "dipside," which is a little ice cream shop with cones, sundaes and malts, all made to order. And the store makes its own ice cream.

Maybe people take it for granted because it's so convenient and ubiquitous, but that blanketing presence is UDF's great advantage and contribution to Cincinnati's taste for sweet cold treats. There are over two hundred UDF

Original Tiffany-style lamps still light the counter at the Oakley Aglamesis in 2019. *Courtesy of Raúl Arias.*

stores, and they're mostly in the Cincinnati area; most are open twenty-four hours a day. The clerks will make you a sundae or a peach shake (in the summer) or a root beer float at 2:00 a.m. if you need it.

UDF's ice cream, like most ice cream, is made in a modern, continuous freezer, so it's lighter and less dense than, say, Graeter's. It's also less expensive. The shops have two lines: one for the regular UDF brand and the other for the Homemade brand, which has less air added and is made with more natural ingredients. UDF's strawberry homemade is made with just cream, milk, sugar and strawberries—some pureed, some still in chunks. The company makes sixty flavors. Brad Lindner, Robert's son, is a part of the third generation of Lindners to run UDF. I haven't heard him use the word *stubborn*, but if that means keeping traditions alive even though it's hard to do so, then this family is stubborn. There aren't many other convenience stores in the country that feature ice cream the way UDF does, and it's a challenge to keep doing it. Most other convenience store employees don't have to know how to make a chocolate soda or a banana split. "It makes training and onboarding a lot more difficult," said Brad Lindner, "but ice cream is at the heart of who we are. It's our identity. "

At Graeter's, Aglamesis and UDF, a rather antique drink is also available. Though it's claimed by New Orleans as its indigenous flavor, nectar soda really comes from Cincinnati. It's a syrup that tastes of bitter almond and vanilla. It's always colored pink and is very sweet. I recommend it at Graeter's, as it makes the prettiest pink ice cream soda.

9

KAFFEE UND KUCHEN AND THE NEIGHBORHOOD BAKERY

The first bite of a Cincinnati schnecken will make you laugh out loud—it's so outrageous. Schnecken may mean snail, but this pastry isn't like any single cinnamon roll spiral. It is three extra-large rolls of enriched sweet dough wrapped around a cinnamon and raisin filling, placed cut-side-up in a loaf pan that already has a quarter of a pound of butter melted in it. After it's baked, all that butter melts into the bread, soaking it about halfway up. You don't eat a whole roll—I don't see how anyone could—you slice it. Many local bakeries make this style of schnecken, but the bakery it's most associated with is the Virginia Bakery, which operated in Clifton for seventy-three years until it closed in 2000.

That closing was a traumatic event for the lovers of sweet baked goods and Cincinnati tradition. Many people cried, as they were not only losing the schnecken that was such an important part of many of their Christmases and Easters, they were also saying goodbye to the most delicious butter bit rolls, butterscotch gems and cookies. The Busken family of Busken Bakery came to the rescue. They are a much larger bakery than Virginia but were friends with the Thies, who owned Virginia Bakery. They got the original recipe (bakers call it a formula) from Tom Thie, made the schnecken at Busken and packaged it in white bakery boxes with the Virginia Bakery logo and red-and-white twine. A sigh of relief was heard around the city. Today, it's sold on holiday occasions.

Cincinnati loves baked goods, especially coffeecakes. I classify schnecken as a kind of coffeecake, though it's different than the more familiar square cake or the rings of laminated dough. I am convinced that no American city boasts more coffeecakes in its neighborhood bakeries than Cincinnati does. For one thing, Cincinnati has a lot of bakeries, including some that are in their third or fourth generations of family ownership. When Wilhelm Gottenbusch, the founder of one of these bakeries, Servatii Pastry Shop, arrived in Cincinnati from Germany in the early 1960s, he said there were two hundred small neighborhood bakeries in the city. That number is now down to twenty or so, but many of those bakeries make ten, fifteen and even thirty different kinds of coffeecake on a rotating basis. The cakes may vary in quality and fanciness, but many of them are really good.

The following are just a few of Cincinnati's bakeries and their most popular cakes: Servatii makes, among other things, plain Danish rings, cinnamon squares, cinnamon pecan squares, cheese pockets, schneckens, cinnamon kringles, fruit crunches, caramel apple crunches, pumpkin spices and coconut cheese squares. Harrison Home Bakery makes double butters, almond pretzels, fruit alligators, cinnamon nut twists, meltaways and tea rings. Busken offers cheesy butterhorns, cinnamon coffeecakes, plain Danish tea rings and raspberry butterhorns. North College Hill Bakery serves breakfast cheesecakes, apricot fruit cakes, cherry fruit cakes, double butters, coconut

Trevor Pascoe places coffeecakes into the oven at North College Hill Bakery in 2017. The bakers start their day at 1:00 a.m. *Courtesy of the* Cincinnati Enquirer *and Meg Vogel.*

raspberry butters, blackberry fruit cakes and Danish cakes like cinnamon apple, butterscotch, cherry crunch, Danish almond ring and cinnamon star stollen. Should I go on? Why so many? Of course, it's a legacy of German culture, but there's a little more to it than that—it's about sharing.

The Germans who crowded into Over-the-Rhine brought with them a tradition from the old country called *Kaffee und Kuchen*, a cherished ritual in Germany. At some time in the afternoon, Germans stop what they're doing and have a cup of coffee and a slice of cake with someone. It could be their family members, co-workers or friends they invite over. That *kuchen* has traditionally been a yeasted cake baked in a square or rectangle, topped with butter or streusel, or maybe fruit and streusel. Germans made that kind of cake synonymous with Cincinnati. In the 1925 edition of *The Fannie Farmer Cookbook*, there's a recipe for a yeasted cake topped with crumbs of butter and sugar. The cake is a streuselkuchen, but in the cookbook, it's called Cincinnati coffee bread. Clementine Paddleford, the well-known national food journalist, made a visit to Cincinnati in the 1950s and was invited to tea with Hattie Thie, the then-owner of the Virginia Bakery. They had a yeasted cinnamon streusel cake, and Paddleford published the recipe as a Cincinnati specialty. If you'd like to try one of these cakes, Graeter's very simple cinnamon streusel is good, and they make a double-butter, like a butterkuchen.

According to *Virginia Bakery Remembered*, early bakers were highly competitive. There were a lot of them packed into the downtown area. For example, around Liberty Street where Wilhelm Thie started his bakery, the bakeries were side by side. There was a great deal of protectiveness about recipes. "If, for example, a baker went out back and saw his son playing with another baker's son, he would run him off. If a baker worked for one company, he would not be hired to work at one of the other bakeries." All of that changed, however, when the important competition was no longer with each other but with supermarkets. At that time, the bakers got together and formed the Cincinnati Retail Baker's Association. Page Busken, the second-generation owner of Busken Bakery, said that a big feature of the association was sharing. If someone invented or discovered a new kind of coffeecake, they'd share the recipe. There was even a Young Baker's Club that came out of the association in the 1950s; there, the sons and grandsons of bakery owners got together and shared formulas and ideas. Joe Busken Sr.'s obituary said that he would hire bakers from Germany; so, he'd get talented bakers, they'd learn from each other and then they would go on to open their own shops. Wilhelm Gottenbusch said Busken helped him a lot when he arrived

A double-butter coffeecake from Graeter's, one of many bakeries that make it. The cake is based on the German butterkuchen. *Courtesy of Raúl Arias.*

in town. "There is a very reciprocal attitude among bakers here. It's just understood that we share. We still all have our signature specialties," said Page Busken for a story I wrote about cheese pockets.

Priscilla Bakery's cheese pockets were shared with other bakers by owner Gordon Nash. They became one of the most popular coffeecakes in the city. Almost every independent baker makes them, or cheese crowns, the individual pastry variation. Cheese pockets are simply squares of pastry with the corners folded in over a filling of sweetened cream or farmer's cheese. Everyone makes them slightly differently; some make them with a lot of cheese, others with powdered sugar, some with sweet dough and others with a Danish dough.

In addition to the one- and two-location bakeries, there are three bakery chains in Cincinnati. One is Graeter's. Though the bakery takes a bit of a backseat to the company's ice cream, it still makes good doughnuts, coffeecakes and birthday cakes. Another multiple-location bakery is Busken, with eight locations; it simultaneously sticks with tradition and stays up to date. Busken was founded in 1928 by Joe Busken and his wife, Daisie. Their oldest son, Joe Jr., joined the bakery in 1953. They did well enough to build a huge central bakery at Madison and Zumstein Streets in Hyde Park, which produced baked goods and was open twenty-four hours a day—it still is. Joe Jr.'s brother Page took the reins in 1970. Dan and Brian Busken are this generation's owners; Dan is the president and Brian is the marketing director. Brian has been behind a number of fun and catchy marketing campaigns, many centered on the bakery's iconic bright-yellow smile cookies, sweet almond-flavored sugar cookies covered with bright-yellow royal icing and a smiley face. They're stamped with the smile design, rather than piped in frosting. The iced and stamped cookies were introduced in the 1960s with seasonal designs like pumpkins. In the 1990s, they added the smile, which has become their signature and a deeply nostalgic taste for many Cincinnatians. The cookies are kept front and center with billboard slogans like "Have a Crumby Day" or "Have an Iced Day."

Servatii was started as a fancy European pastry shop. Within a short time of moving to Cincinnati, I came across the bakery's macaroons at a party, which convinced me I had made a good choice for a new home. These are unlike other cookies called macaroons; they are shortbread cookies topped with an almond paste layer, a rum-flavored chocolate layer and a chocolate coating.

Greg Gottenbusch of Servatii Pastry Shop & Deli at the Servatii Pastry Shop in Symmes Township in 2017. *Courtesy of the* Cincinnati Enquirer *and Meg Vogel.*

Other independent bakeries in Cincinnati include the BonBonerie, which has been making delicious pastries in O'Bryonville since 1983. They make beautiful decorated cookies, cakes, scones and coffeecakes in their sweet-smelling shop, where everything is pretty from the doilies to the decorations on the cakes. The bakery's opera cream torte is worth a special mention. It's based on an opera cream candy that's a favorite Cincinnati chocolate. It appeared in the 1920s and was probably invented by the Putnam Candy Company. It's very simple, taste-wise; it has a creamy vanilla filling, a soft fondant and is enrobed in chocolate—either dark or milk. Any candy store that still makes candy from scratch has a selection of these opera cream candies. In 1984, a customer asked the bakery to make a cake based on the candy. BonBonerie's torte takes the candy's two simple components and renders them in a moist dark chocolate cake with a dense and sweet vanilla filling. It used to be on many restaurant dessert menus, and it still is, though you come across it less. You can either buy or order them at the BonBonerie Café, which still occupies just one location.

BonBonerie owners Mary Pat Pace (*left*) and Sharon Butler (*right*) holding an opera cream cake, celebrating thirty years in business in 2013. *Courtesy of the* Cincinnati Enquirer *and Leigh Taylor.*

Brown Bear Bakery doesn't have any direct connection to the cozy cafés and living rooms where German Cincinnatians drank coffee and ate kuchen together. However, it is a cozy space in Over-the-Rhine, across the street from St. Mary's Church, the oldest operating church in Cincinnati (dedicated in 1842), where they still have mass in Latin and German—so it does bring those days to mind. And the baked goods that Blair Fornshell makes at Brown Bear, like ginger cookies and the best cinnamon rolls, along with croissants and other layered pastries, are homey and rich lovely

The cozy little bakeries and cafés where German Cincinnatians ate coffeecake together changed as the nineteenth century moved on. The small businesses that knit the German community together gave way to a much larger production business that ended up making some of the Germans and Cincinnati famous.

10

BEER

Twice the National Average

It was 1981, the dark days for good American beer; Budweiser and Miller ruled the brewing world. The hundreds of regional beer brands that had once offered alternatives to what was advertised on television had dwindled. But in Cincinnati, where brand loyalty is strong, there were still a few local breweries: Hudepohl, Schoenling and Wiedemann. They were remnants of a once-mighty local beer economy. That year, in an attempt to distinguish themselves from bigger competitors, Hudepohl did something new—and old. The brewery introduced a beer that was darker, with more body and flavor than the big beers, something more like an imported beer. It was named for a long-dead Bavarian immigrant, the biggest beer baron who had ever rolled out a barrel in Cincinnati: Christian Moerlein. The brewery used an old Moerlein logo and brewed the beer without any adjuncts, such as rice or wheat. The beer passed the German purity law, the Reinheitsgebot (which only allows the use of water, hops, malt and yeast).

The general manager of Hudepohl, who came up with the idea, was Bob Pohl, the grandson of Louis Hudepohl, the brewery's founder. He had no illusions that this kind of beer could replace the popular light beers that most people drank. The brewery aimed the beer at a niche market: mostly men, aged eighteen to thirty-five, who were well educated and had a high income. They introduced it by delivering the first batch to Arnold's Bar and Grill in a horse-drawn cart. The beer did well, selling more than double what the brewery expected. The next year, Hudepohl widened distribution and added two more beers: a bock and an Oktoberfest. The beer was a resurrection, but it was ahead of its time. The brewery called it super-premium (it cost $2.99 per six-pack), but it was a craft beer before there was such a thing.

That was the first time that Cincinnati's rich beer history got tapped as an inspiration for something new. Thirty years later, that history was once again called on. The city's past was the underpinning that brought meaning and a local flavor to the craft beer movement as it developed in Cincinnati. And Christian Moerlein, again, provided the inspiration.

In 2004, Greg Hardman was the CEO of Warsteiner Importers Agency—a good gig. The company had even moved its headquarters from Chicago to Cincinnati so that he could run the company from home. But that year, Hardman quit his job. Like many intrepid Cincinnatians before him, he had decided to go into the brewery business. His plan was to honor all those who'd made beer here and to bring back Cincinnati's glory days as a brewing city.

The 1981 Christian Moerlein brew hadn't saved Hudepohl. In 1986, it was bought by Schoenling, the maker of Little Kings, to become the Hudepohl-Schoenling Brewing Co. The brewery lasted for a while, making beer in Schoenling's Central Parkway brewery, but it sold the facility to the Boston Beer Company, which then brewed for them on contract. In 2004,

The first batch of the revived Christian Moerlein lager was delivered to Arnold's Café by horse-drawn wagon in 1981. *Courtesy of the* Cincinnati Enquirer *and Jeff Hinckley.*

Faux monks pulling the Moerlein Trojan goat in the 2016 Bockfest Parade. A mural of James Brown, who recorded in Cincinnati, can be seen in the background. *Courtesy of the* Cincinnati Enquirer *and Madison Schmidt.*

Boston Beer ended the contract, and in an affront to hometown pride, the beers were brewed in Pennsylvania and Wisconsin. They were the last beers standing from a proud tradition in Cincinnati—a dribble that was almost dry when compared to the flowing torrents of golden beer from one hundred years earlier.

Hardman bought Hudepohl-Schoenling and vowed to bring its beers back to Cincinnati, where they would once again be brewed in their hometown, where their loyal fans lived and drank. Hardman called his new company Christian Moerlein Brewing after the man and the best beer he'd just bought. Hardman then owned the logos, marketing rights and recipes for sixty-five brands, including Christian Moerlein Lager, Oktoberfest and Bock; Hudepohl Amber; Hudy Delight; and Burger. He added Schoenling's Little Kings brand, the cream ale in green seven-ounce bottles, in 2008.

It's amazing that the brands still existed at all. Half of Cincinnati's brewing story was one of prosperity and growth, of scores of breweries and of fortunes made. The other half was a decline caused by the temperance movement, a mistrust of Germans during World War I, Prohibition, the consolidation of big beer at the expense of small local brands and the dumbing-down of Americans' tastes. It is another testament to Cincinnatians' hometown loyalties that they were still drinking Hudepohl from a brewery that was founded in 1885 and started up again after Prohibition.

Hardman's purchase was made as the national craft beer movement was really taking off. It was well underway in San Francisco, Portland and some other parts of the country, including Boston, where the Boston Beer Company (the brewer of Sam Adams) had gone public in 1995. That brewery had its own Cincinnati resurrection story. The Boston Beer Company actually brewed quite a bit of its beer in Cincinnati, but because the brand was so closely tied to Boston, it didn't publicize it. Boston Beer's owner, Jim Koch, grew up in Cincinnati, and his father and grandfather had been brewers in Cincinnati breweries. He used his family's recipe to brew the first Sam Adams beer.

As the craft beer movement was getting started in the 2000s and 2010s, some Cincinnatians were developing a strong interest in the city's beer history. This was partly due to interest in the area of the city where beer had been made, the Brewery District of Over-the-Rhine, where hulks of old breweries reminded us of the past. People were busy renovating old buildings, discovering their history and revealing huge cellars deep under the foundations that were parts of old breweries. Everything was coming together to make beer history relevant. Among the people participating in the new-old beer craze was Mike Morgan, a lawyer and real estate agent involved in the development of the brewery district and in telling the history of Cincinnati beer. He is also the author of *Cincinnati Beer*. That history, I'm sure it's not surprising to hear, is intermingled with the German history of Cincinnati. The Germans not only made contributions as enthusiastic drinkers of beer, but they also made contributions as brewers, particularly with an innovation that popularized beer for everyone.

The history of Cincinnati beer goes back almost to the founding of the city. The first major brewer in the city was J. Walker Company, which made English- and Scottish-style ales. An ale, like all beers, is made by first soaking and sprouting barley, kilning it to stop the sprouting, then milling it, mixing with water and boiling it. (In Cincinnati, breweries used river water unless they had a well.) Then, it was set to ferment at room temperature, usually after adding older beer. Brewers didn't know at the time that the older beer contained yeast; they just knew that it worked. Once the yeast started digesting the sugars in the malt and creating both alcohol and carbon dioxide for fizz, the beer was ready to be kegged or bottled, where it fermented a bit more.

Moerlein's graphic. *Courtesy of the Library of Congress, artist unknown.*

The Germans' arrival in Cincinnati en masse started in the 1840s, coinciding with the discovery of what yeast actually was and with the discovery of different strains of yeast. One of these strains was lager yeast; it worked differently than ale yeast, as it worked from the bottom instead of floating on top. Lager yeast also had to ferment at very chilly temperatures, almost freezing. It also had to be "lagered," or stored, at cold temps, from thirty-four to thirty-six degrees Fahrenheit. But the beer it made was so lovely, crisp, light, easy to drink, refreshing and foamy.

Pilsner Urquell, a lager, was brewed in Czechoslovakia in 1844, and the lager yeast came to the United States several years later. Morgan discounts some claims that lager was made in Cincinnati in the 1840s; he thinks that Cincinnati started making lager around 1850. In that year, there were sixteen breweries in town, including those in Newport and Covington. By 1855 there were thirty-four, with lager to thank for it. Cincinnati, along with the rest of the country, was enamored of this delicious, crisp beer. Various breweries, which were all owned by Germans, began making thousands of gallons of lager. Before mechanical refrigeration was introduced in the 1880s, it was mostly brewed in the winter, but lager was also fermented and stored underground in cave-like rooms that were kept cold with ice. In Over-the-Rhine, brewers began digging, either straight down or, as they did on the northern edges of Over-the-Rhine, laterally, into the hill that rose up from the basin.

From the 1850s to 1919, lagers made a number of Cincinnatians millionaires, employed thousands of people and attracted visitors to the city. Herancourt was the first large-scale lager brewery. The brewery started to brew lager in 1855, and in four years, it went from making two thousand to four thousand barrels a year. By 1878, the brewery was making one hundred thousand barrels a year. It was a major industry in Cincinnati, and old photos and drawings of the brewery buildings show substantial brick buildings, often designed in the Rundbogenstil or German Romanesque Revival style, which made them look like castles.

Christian Moerlein, founded in 1873, was the most successful brewery in terms of numbers of barrels. It grew to be the largest brewer in Ohio. The list of Moerlein's fellow beer barons is long and Teutonic: John Hauck, Louis Hudepohl, Conrad Windisch, John Kauffman and George Weber. Though they tended to come from the lower classes in Germany, in the United States they were beer barons, pillars of the community. They contributed to the zoo, the arts and Turner Halls. (Though Morgan gets a little impatient with their portrayal as perfect citizens, and he has a chapter titled "The Second Generation Wrecks the Family Business.")

Now, German Cincinnatians could drink all the beer they wanted—and they wanted a lot. They drank in biergartens, saloons and bars; they drank during the week, and they drank on Sunday. In fact, they particularly liked drinking on Sunday. On Continental Sunday, whole families went to one of the biergartens, like Wielert's or Schniesing's, after church. And the presence of all the fun-loving, beer-powered venues attracted non-Germans to Vine Street, a major north–south route from the city through Over-the-Rhine (see chapter 11). In 1893, the average consumption of beer in the United States was sixteen gallons per capita. In Cincinnati, it was forty—more than twice the national average.

All of this, and especially the particular habit of drinking on Sunday, brought Cincinnati into conflict with a gathering temperance movement, the movement that came before Prohibition in the United States. Its purpose was to warn of the evils of alcohol, to get Americans to drink less and to regulate when, where and how alcohol, including beer, could be made and

Above: Weidemann's Brewery in Newport, a small part of its very large complex. *Courtesy of the* Cincinnati Enquirer.

Opposite: Print of a bartender from 1889, during the time Vine Street was at its busiest. *Courtesy of a Library of Congress bartender.*

sold. Well, Germans didn't like being told not to drink. In fact, the freedom-lovers who had come from Germany after fighting repressive regimes didn't really like being told what to do at all. In the 1880s, when temperance was turning into prohibition, the country divided into "drys" and "wets." Most urban immigrants and Catholics, including Germans, were on the "wet" side, while pious Protestant groups and women were on the "dry" side, along with Nativists (the Know-Nothing Party), who associated beer and drinking with ethnic groups they didn't like. There was a prevalent stereotype that

Our Beloved German-American, a cartoon from *Puck*, 1900. The artist was Udo J Keppler. "He would have a happier time if he looked through American-made spectacles." *Courtesy of J. Ottmann Lith. Co., Library of Congress.*

described Germans as portly, sausage-eating drunkards whose real loyalty was to their fatherland. The brewing industry helped support the anti-prohibition cause—that is, until World War I.

When Germany went to war with England and France, most German-Americans were vocally on Germany's side, confirming suspicions of disloyalty. They were shocked when the United States got into the war on England and France's side. Though many changed their alliances to their new country, there was a backlash against them. This period is often referred to as one of "hysteria," and it was certainly a time when protecting civil rights seemed less important than protecting perceived national security and getting everyone to toe the patriotic line. The government came down very hard on Germans, and popular sentiment went against them. In Cincinnati, streets were renamed, teachers were fired and teaching the German language was forbidden.

Not long after the Armistice was signed on November 11, 1918, Prohibition began. It lasted for thirteen years and effectively killed a thriving industry, put an end to the good times in Cincinnati's many saloons and tore down one of the city's thriving economic engines. It turned some people (bootleggers) rich, helped the rise of organized crime and was generally considered a failed experiment, though it did succeed in getting people to drink less.

One brewery, Bruckmann, survived Prohibition without closing down; this was mostly because it began making "medicinal" low-alcohol "near-beer" and soft drinks. Four breweries, including Hudepohl, were able to start again, but the city's breweries were never the same. Reviving the breweries of Cincinnati was difficult because they all tended to be right in the middle of an urban area that had been repurposed during the dry decade. Beer technology had progressed in the rest of the world, making it expensive to retool and become competitive. Cincinnati lost out against breweries from Milwaukee and St. Louis that used economies of scale and aggressive marketing to dominate. To skip across the decades, those other brands became monsters, and the lagers got lighter and less flavorful, as they started using adjuncts like rice and wheat. This all created a bleak landscape of mediocre beer for most of the rest of the century. In 2010, three companies controlled 80 percent of beer sales, and it all tasted the same. Like so many things, from the mid-twentieth century on, beer was industrialized and dumbed down, just like ice cream, tomatoes and fast-food restaurants. Of course, people longed for something better, more interesting and local.

This is when craft beer came on the scene. The first stage of the local craft beer movement (besides the first Christian Moerlein relaunch—a somewhat unique case) was the brewpub, where beer was made on-site and served with food. Oldenburg Brewery in Fort Mitchell, Kentucky, opened in 1987 and made some German-style lagers; it closed, however, in 2001, after having educated a bunch of Cincinnatians in the virtues of small-batch beer. The Barrel House in Over-the-Rhine was a significant early brewpub. It opened in 1994, when the neighborhood was starting to feature a nightlife, but the area was still old, run-down and scary to many outsiders, especially after the unrest of 2001. The Barrel House closed in 2005. Then, the chain micropub Rock Bottom opened on Fountain Square, making only-in-Cincinnati beers, and the first Hofbräuhaus outside of Munich opened in 2003 in Newport.

Cincinnati had been celebrating one kind of beer in a quirky, grassroots way since 1992, when Bockfest was founded. The festival started as a promotional event for another revival beer from Hudepohl-Schoenling: the Christian Moerlein Bock beer. Traditionally, it's the beer that monks drink to sustain themselves during Lent. Bockfest was a party around a parade. Held during Lent, the parade started at Arnold's Bar and Grill and ended at Old St. Mary's in Over-the-Rhine, the city's oldest church. It consisted of people dressed as monks, a Trojan goat and a big bock hall celebration—overall a goofy, fun way to celebrate beer, Cincinnati and German heritage. It has only gotten bigger since that time. Jim Tarbell, an aficionado of all things historic Cincinnati, is always in the front of the parade, in Renaissance costume, which he said was "as much privilege as anyone could want in a lifetime." In 2017, twenty-five thousand people participated in Bockfest.

In Cincinnati, and nationally, the brewpub fad faded. The second wave of local beers grew out of the fad of home brewing, which had been federally legalized in 1978. Dan Listermann opened a brewing supply company near Xavier University in the early 1990s, including his own invention for better bottling. Home brew clubs, like the Bloatarians and the Malt Infusers, became quite active at this time. Then home brewers went commercial. In 2005, Mike Dewey, a home brewer, and his wife, Kathleen, opened Mount Carmel Brewery in an old farmhouse on the far east side of town. Home brewers Jason Roeper and Randy Schiltz opened Rivertown in 2009. Blank Slate opened in 2011, and Fifty West opened in 2012.

By 2013, Christian Moerlein had brought its production back to Cincinnati, where it was bottling new beers in its facility at the old Kauffman Brewery in Over-the-Rhine. The brewery had also been making microbrews in their restaurant and brewpub, the Moerlein Lager House, which had opened along with a new park on the riverfront. It had great views of the Suspension Bridge, a lot of new Moerlein beers, along with others, and plenty of beer memorabilia. Hardman had not reached 1 percent of the beer market, as he had boldly claimed he would. As it turns out, he had a lot of competition.

Part of the neighborhood revival of Over-the-Rhine was the walking tours from American Legacy Tours, which took people down into the lager tunnels and caves. The tours helped people picture and appreciate the city's beer history. One of the little harassing laws leading up to Prohibition was that you couldn't brew and bottle beer in the same facility, so some breweries connected those two facilities with under-the-street tunnels. Each new discovery brought a little more attention. The Bockfest got bigger without losing its quirk.

In 2013, the State of Ohio changed its licensing fees for microbreweries. Before, it cost $3,906 for a full A1A license, which a bar would get if it wanted to open a room where people could come taste beer; after, it went down to $1,000.

MadTree opened in 2013 in the Pleasant Ridge area; the brewery went all in and started canning beer. It later opened a tasting room that got so full you couldn't park nearby. Then Rhinegeist opened a cavernous brewery in Over-the-Rhine, in the former Moerlein Brewery. It was truly in the Brewery District, north of Liberty Street, with a new streetcar stop right in front. Patrons entered through what looked like an industrial warehouse and walked up three flights of rough stairs to a huge room that, once it got popular, had off-the-chart decibels. MadTree later moved to a larger facility in Oakley, which still filled to the brim.

Once the craft beer momentum started, it snowballed. Mike Dewey said in a newspaper article in 2015 that it was "the dot-com era of beer." The Reds added local craft brew to their beer lineup. Kroger started buying local beer, and Jungle Jim's, the gigantic local grocery store with two locations, always stocked it all. Oktoberfest and Taste of Cincinnati featured plenty of local beers. Tasting rooms got more elaborate; instead of a few hand-labeled taps, there was food, tours and televisions, just like a bar. Taft's Ale House opened in 2015, in a stunning new space in Over-the-Rhine; it was not a former brewery but a former church that was gorgeously redone, with beer tanks in place of the altar. Urban Artifact opened in Northside to make sour beers with brewers interested in wild yeasts.

By 2018, the retail slots were full, and it became unlikely that anyone new would break into selling craft beer in retail outlets in Cincinnati. "The era of moving from a microbrewery to a multi-state regional is not dead, but it's going to be very infrequent," said Burt Watson, chief economist for the Brewers Association, in 2017. At that point, 80 percent of beer-drinking adults in the United States lived within ten miles of a brewery. Probably the last brewery to open big and try to get in on distribution was Braxton in Covington, Kentucky.

Today, any ambitious brewer has to open a pub with beer and food, so new breweries became more like the brewpubs of the 1990s. They opened all over town to serve neighborhoods instead of distributors. They included Woodburn in Walnut Hills; Nine Giant in Pleasant Ridge; Brink in College Hill; Fretboard in Blue Ash; Darkness in Bellevue, Kentucky. Sam Adams finally opened a tasting room in 2018, across from its large-scale brewing facility near Findlay Market. Here, the company has a nano brewery to try new styles and tap some specialty beers that aren't available in stores.

As of 2019, there were more than fifty craft breweries in the Greater Cincinnati area. Moerlein continues to emphasize its link to the past in its Over-the-Rhine taproom in the former Kauffman Malt House with its Saturday Night Singalongs and Weinerwurst Mike Food Counter. Another heritage beer brand, Wiedemann, has been revived by the Newberry family. Though it had been made in Northern Kentucky, the new brewery and beer garden opened in St. Bernard in a former funeral home.

The Christian Moerlein taproom in the former Kauffman Malt House, Over-the-Rhine, in 2019. *Courtesy of Raúl Arias.*

The Over-the-Rhine Heritage Brewery District, founded in 2003, pushes for preservation of the largest collection of pre-Prohibition breweries in the country. And it strives to develop the neighborhood for residential and commercial use. There are forty-seven buildings from fourteen breweries that still exist in the northern part of Over-the-Rhine. The Brewing Heritage Trail, which was unveiled in 2018, winds through the Brewery District and features virtual tours, public art and bronze medallions that mark the way. The trail's plan for the neighborhood has become part of the comprehensive plan for the city.

It's interesting and a little ironic that the craft beer revolution mirrored, in reverse, the lager revolution that took place between the 1850s and 1920. The lager that had made so many German Cincinnatians rich was popular for its lightness and "quaff-ability," an improvement on heavier, less consistent ales that came before it. But lager became so light and characterless that the beer lovers of the 1990s–2020 made their own revolution by reversing the trend and making ales that had character, body, variation and quirkiness.

11

PLAYING UNDER THE BRIGHT LIGHTS OF VINE STREET

The pedal wagons showed up on Vine Street in 2012. Like a bicycle built for thirteen—with cup holders—the human-propelled party vehicles became a favorite of bachelorette parties and other lubricated groups of friends who drink beer, sing songs and whoop it up while pedaling past blocks of bars, restaurants and Washington Park.

It would have been impossible to imagine something like this existing just fifteen years earlier. Vine Street is one of the main arteries of the city, running from Second Street, through downtown, north through Over-the-Rhine, up the hill, to Clifton and even farther north. The section of the street that runs through Over-the-Rhine, between Central Parkway and Liberty Street, once went past blocks of boarded-up nineteenth-century buildings. At one time, if you looked up, you could see the buildings' Italianate flourishes and details, but at street level, they were crumbling and empty. Just a block to the west, Washington Park was home to drug users, alcoholics and the homeless. But Cincinnati's urban renaissance of the 2010s is now evident in this neighborhood. A combination of government and private investment from the Cincinnati City Center Development Corporation, along with a new interest in urban living and historic renovation, has filled up the vacant buildings and injected millions of dollars into the neighborhood. Its success created fast-forwarded development in which pedal wagons are an almost surreal feature.

But if you could go back 120 to 140 years ago, those pedal wagons would have fit right in—actually, they would have been tame. Vine Street

Pedal wagons began operating in Over-the-Rhine in 2012. *Courtesy of Carol Highsmith, Library of Congress.*

in the 1870s to 1920 was a wide-open entertainment district where the beer flowed, the dance halls were full, orchestras played, families sat in beer gardens and men put their feet up on the brass rails at multiple saloons. The Vine Street of today, with its mix of casual bars and restaurants, recapitulates that old history.

In the 1880s, Cincinnati was expanding into a new metropolis with the annexation of surrounding communities. Public transit was moving people away from the original city in the "basin" to new neighborhoods and suburbs on the hillsides. The old, snug taverns of Over-the-Rhine were being replaced by saloons, bars and beer gardens. It was a chaotic era, and one thing that grew out of it was the political boss system. Cincinnati had a classic behind-the-scenes boss, George Cox. He wielded much of his power from a table at Wielert's at the corner of Vine and Fourteenth Streets, one of the many German beer halls in Over-the-Rhine.

Wielert's is the setting in the first scene of *Back Street*, Fannie Hurst's novel about the long-suffering mistress of a married man. Hurst, a hugely successful novelist of women's fiction in the 1920s and 1930s, was born in the nearby city of Hamilton and knew Cincinnati well. She described the beer hall's patrons:

> *Families that dined out once a week. Sturdy, unstylish women with enormous busts, who ate and drank with relish, but knew, to a penny, for how much less they could spread their groaning home-tables with these luxuries of Schmierkase and Schnittlauch, bratwurst that had been fried without a prong of the exploring fork puncturing the sausage-casing for loss of juice. Solid, thrifty men, in gates-ajar collars and congress shoes, to whom the Turnverein and Sangverein, the right lager, the virtuous wife, the virgin daughter, the respecting son, the well-tended business, were universe.* [Schmierkase and schnittlauch is cottage cheese with chives.]

But Vine Street's reputation rested on the more raucous nightlife that developed from the German neighborhood. The *WPA Guide to Cincinnati* described it in nostalgic terms.

> *Old-timers turn dewy-eyed as they recite the glories of Vine Street. They remember the beer-gardens and concert-halls, the burlesque houses and variety shows, the shooting galleries and bowling alleys: orchestras everywhere and everybody singing "Boom-Ta-Ra" and "It's a Daisy." They have not forgotten the brazen signs announcing, "Free Wienerwurst with Every Drink," nor the aproned waiters dashing about, an incredible array of mugs in their hands.*

Vine Street also attracted lots of non-Germans. The area's Germanness may have become somewhat kitschy over time; it was a sort of Bourbon Street, a magnet for traveling salesmen and visitors to the Queen City. The stories about it are colored with nostalgia, and the tall tales about epic drinking exploits were told in the decade of Prohibition, when an intense nostalgia set in about a way of life that ended so abruptly. *Pioneers of Night Life on Vine Street* by Frank Grayson, a compilation of columns he wrote in the *Cincinnati Times-Star*, was published as a book in 1924. In the book, Grayson painted a vivid picture of Vine Street (he variously called it the Bubbling Boulevard, the Rialto and the Old Strasse). He wrote of "sassy cut-ups," who could drink seventy-five beers in a night, which surely is an exaggeration, even if Cincinnati did drink twice the national average. He wrote about "the yeasty foam," "the old lager," "the amber," the nectar, the "stuff that made Cincinnati even more famous than Milwaukee" and "the tall ones." At that time, beer came in scuttles, schooners, pipes and hatfuls.

Wielert's, a respectable German beer and dance hall on Vine Street, where musicians played and Boss Cox ran the city. *Courtesy of the* Cincinnati Enquirer.

Young men smoking outside a saloon tied to the Herancourt Brewery. *Courtesy of the Public Library of Cincinnati and Hamilton County.*

> *Night life on Vine Street in its golden days was like a plate of steaming hash. Why? Because it had everything in it to make it palatable. I do not believe that any city in the United States, or, perhaps, in the whole world could point with pride to a thoroughfare that held such a fascination for those who liked to play around under the bright lights, as did Vine Street to the red-blooded youth and elders of three decades ago or so.*
>
> *Vine Street stood supreme in the diversity of its sporting life; in the thistledown lightness of its night life, in its Bohemian atmosphere; in the picturesqueness and humor of numerous of its habitués and in the variety of charm of its entertainment.*

Vine Street didn't just have drinking; there was the food—hearty, German food mostly, including the cheap lunches that were served free with beer. These lunches were usually served at "tied" houses, where only one brewery's products were sold. An *Enquirer* article from 1887 described these free lunches: "Sample rooms generally set a lunch of roast beef, olives, crackers and cheese. The beer saloons always offer greasy food and salt fish of some kind. It is cut in chunks and piled on a big platter, on others are chopped herring, anchovies, Russian sardines, black bread in pieces an inch square, big fat white radishes, potato salad, pumpernickel, blood pudding cut in slices." John Hauck, the beer baron, used to have lunch at a Hauck's Brewery every day, as described in the *Serene Cincinnatians*: "He would buy a nickel schooner of suds and eat a man's size—a big man's size—of the free lunch, with never a thought of the humor of the situation, though it did occur, wryly, to the saloon keeper." Hauck also owned the Reds at one time and essentially turned the team's ballpark into a "tied house," where only Hauck's beer was served along with sausage.

Grayson remembers when "the steam was arising from the roast of beef, filling the nostrils with its seductive aroma, and the spaghetti was just a-writhing in its bowl for someone to come along and give it a home." He said he would give his "right eye at this very moment just for five minutes of the days of old—just long enough, in fact, to surround a sliced tongue sandwich, embellished with cottage cheese and to wash it down with a standpipe of John Hauck's." He continued, "As long as I am here to encumber the Earth, the memory of that combination shall never die." He asked, "What would you give if you could sit down again in front of a stack of potato pancakes like those that John B. Wolke used to deal to his customers at his café on upper Vine Street?" He also remembered the mobile vendors of food who would push carts or carry baskets up and down the street, selling to the merrymakers.

Above: Fifth and Vine, known as the Nasty Corner, a notorious collection of saloons and bars offering beer and a free lunch. *The Cincinnati Enquirer.*

Left: A poster advertising the musical show *A Hot Old Time* in 1902. It uses well-worn stereotypes of Germans and their love for beer and sausages. *Courtesy of the U.S Lithographic Co., Russel-Morgan Print, Library of Congress.*

> *What has become of the tamale man with his basket, his spotted white apron and his steaming can? They used to be as plentiful on Vine Street as raspberries along a rail fence. What was a more fitting climax to a moist evening than to meet up with one of these fellahs and peel off a couple of those tamales? They were a positive tonic. They made you want to go back from whence you came, which, in nine cases out of ten, was a gilded palace of suds. A tamale at two or three in the morning was delicious. Especially good when you had about 75 beers under your belt. Above that number, they weren't so good.*

Wienerwursts were perhaps the most distinctive food of Vine Street; they were given away at saloons and sold on the street.

> *It seemed as if every vendor of frankfurters, bratwursts and wieners in Over-the-Rhine was known as Wienerwurst Mike. One of these Mikes, basket on one arm and can of steaming wieners on the other, was a nightly visitor at the Over-the-Rhine resorts. I can close my eyes now and hear him thumping across the floors on that wooden leg.*

Another midnight purveyor of food was Simon, the hot corn man.

> *He had a way of boiling the corn in the husk, and with each ear of corn, he handed out a substance that passed as butter. Then, he would give the customer a knife with which to spread the butter on the corn. There were a lot of greasy maps decorating Vine Street in the wake of Simon.*

Grayson also remembered pig knuckles and pigs' feet, Bermuda onion and the beef steak smothered with onions, served in a "fetching and seductive way" by Schwind's Place on the west side of Vine Street, which was also noted for its German fried potatoes and potato pancakes. There was Cramer's Lobster and Frog Place and the Atlantic Garden, which slipped into seediness well before Prohibition put it out of business. (Atlantic Garden was half of a famous battle in which two bars shot fireworks across the street at each other.)

Temperance was the first phase of the movement that ended in Prohibition. As Michael Morgan, the author of *Cincinnati Beer*, said, "It was a lobbying group that had political power despite the fact that most Americans didn't want it." Temperance was a Christian movement that was mostly led by women and clergymen who were fighting what were, in fact, serious social problems caused by the heavy drinking of the early nineteenth century. Temperance activists first tried "moral suasion," like when "women's crusades" of weeping and praying women entered saloons. Mothers encouraged their sons to "take the pledge" that they would never drink. But as the century went on, reformers turned to legal prohibitions, partly because new immigrants from Ireland and Germany were not so easily swayed by appeals to morality. Carrie Nation, the well-known anti-drinking activist, was known for attacking saloons with her hatchet. There's a commonly told story that she said she started out to attack the saloons on Vine Street but didn't because she "would have dropped of exhaustion before [she'd] gone a block." However, she probably never said this. Greg Hand, a Cincinnati history blogger, has tried to confirm the quote but can find no Cincinnati papers that reported the quote when Nation was here.

The crusaders against drinking finally won their fight when Prohibition went into effect in 1920. Drinking went underground—no more bright lights on Vine Street. However, if you were lucky, you may have been invited to a party at the Marble Palace, the mansion built by notorious bootlegger George Remus in Price Hill. At one lavish event that was thrown for one

"Woman's Crusade against Temperance," or "You Shust Git Out," which was presumably what the female bar owner was telling the weeping crusaders. Photograph by C.S. Reinhart and printed in *Harper's Weekly* in 1874. *Courtesy of the Library of Congress.*

Busy Vine Street in 1970. *Courtesy of the* Cincinnati Enquirer *and Tom Hubbard.*

hundred couples on New Year's Eve 1922, the party favors were diamond stickpins for the men and brand-new cars for the women. Remus was an outsized figure; there's even a bourbon named for him. Though the history section of the company's website details his story, it leaves out the part where he murdered his wife.

Vine Street's prosperity then followed the fate of its Over-the-Rhine neighborhood for the rest of the twentieth century. By 2000, Vine Street was the main corridor through a crumbling neighborhood. People still called it home, but the vacancy rate in the neighborhood was very high. There was almost no market rate housing. Crime was high, and perception of crime by people who lived in other parts of the city was even higher. After 3CDC refurbished Fountain Square and the area around it, it focused on Vine Street north of Central Parkway and began, in a very methodical way, developing northward on Vine Street, buying buildings and finding tenants. The group also supervised the renovation of Washington Park, across from Music Hall. The park was transformed from a hangout for the homeless and addicted to a beautiful park that attracted people from the neighborhood as well as people from the rest of the city. It all started a rapid and successful remaking of Over-the-Rhine. After many years of city-wide arguing and wrangling, a streetcar opened that went from the Ohio River, through downtown and Over-the-Rhine, to Findlay Market.

Vine Street began coming back to life. In 2008, Jean-Robert de Cavel, who owned several French restaurants downtown, stuck his neck out and opened a restaurant in an old laundromat on Vine Street, just north of Thirteenth Street, and called it Lavomatic. In 2010, Daniel Wright, a chef from Chicago, opened Senate across the street. "When Dan decided on Over-the-Rhine as a location for Senate, I was absolutely 100 percent against it," said his wife, Lana Shteiwi Wright, in a cookbook they later published. "It was dangerous. It was a ghost of a neighborhood, but he saw something that I couldn't see because he didn't have a history with it. He could see the area was going to develop." Senate did well; it was crowded on its opening day and has been ever since.

Senate had fun, approachable food that was also quite sophisticated. Hot dogs were the big draw there and caused the biggest buzz. I don't know if Wright thought of this, but he had become the new Wienerwurst Mike of Vine Street. After Senate had been open for a few years, Wright and his wife opened Abigail Street next door. Lana Shteiwi Wright was born to a Jordanian family who owned Gold Star Chili franchises, and the new restaurant featured Middle Eastern food inspired by her background. Later came Pontiac, a barbecue restaurant.

Lackman Bar, named for an old brewery, opened in 2011. Taste of Belgium opened a café with a long list of Belgian and craft beers and a Belgian menu. Two brothers who had opened a successful pizza pop-up opened A Tavola with a wood-fired pizza oven from Italy and began making authentic Neapolitan pizza. The Thunderdome Group, which was owned by brothers Joe and John Lanni and Alex Blust, opened a taco and bourbon restaurant with an outlaw country theme called Bakersfield. They subsequently became the most successful owners on Vine Street and became anchors in the development. They opened a burger restaurant next door called Krueger's and a fried chicken restaurant called the Eagle. An offshoot of the Eagle was a chicken finger carry-out called City Bird. They then added Pepp and Dolores, an inexpensive Italian restaurant, to their list of restaurants. They continued to open more locations of Bakersfield and the Eagle in other Midwestern cities.

The juxtaposition of the old Over-the-Rhine and the new Over-the-Rhine is not always easy. There are resentments from residents who feel their neighborhood has been changed without their consent, and now, real estate prices and rents are pricing them out.

Vine Street filled with diners and strollers walking between the bars and restaurants in 2019. *Courtesy of Raúl Arias.*

Vine Street stood in contrast to another development, the Banks, which was on the riverfront between the Great American Ballpark and Paul Brown Stadium. It, too, was in close proximity to a beautiful new park and public investment, but its tenants were more likely to be chain restaurants of a high quality, like Ruth's Chris and Yard House (for a while, Toby Keith's I Love This Bar and Grill was also a tenant). It was an all-new construction, so instead of being inspired by history, the Banks started fresh, without the constraints of the older, smaller buildings on Vine Street. It ended up being rather characterless and would not look out of place in any suburban development. It has not been as successful as Vine Street, with a lot of restaurant turnover, and while traffic on game days is good, it is not as busy the rest of the time.

While the restaurants on Vine Street are not chains, almost none of them are anything like old-guard fine dining (the Mercer is the closest to that style). They are Cincinnati's somewhat belated expression of the culinary revolution that has been happening all over the United States. They are casual but take food seriously; they don't take reservations and are often quite small. They play with culinary traditions, pay homage to the past, reflect or at least fit into the neighborhood and offer a new style of dining that appeals to millennials in particular. It is about not planning ahead, but it often makes a night of eating and drinking in different places, and with a party of people who has different needs, possible.

Because these restaurants don't take reservations but are often full, people often put their name on a list and go to a bar or another restaurant and put their names on a list there. It has created a kind of roaming, public atmosphere. It isn't quite the Gay Nineties of the nineteenth century, but there was more street activity at that time than Cincinnati had seen since the days of saloons and beer halls.

12

CINCINNATI'S THREE WAY

Our Chili

While Graeter's ice cream, goetta and other unique Cincinnati foods have become interesting to people from other places, the city's most distinctive food often doesn't get much respect from out-of-towners and writers. For instance, in 2013, the satirical sports website Deadspin published a list rating regional food from every state. They rated Cincinnati chili in fifty-second place, with fifty-first place being a car wreck. The writer hated the chili for its taste, which is okay, though sad for him. And there's no indication that he ever actually tried it. Here's what he was especially vitriolic about:

> *Whatever virtue this bad-tasting Z-grade atrocity once contained derived from its exemplification of a set of certain cherished American fables—immigrant ingenuity, the cultural melting pot, old things combining into new things—and has now been totally swamped and consumed by different and infinitely uglier American realities: the commodification of culture; the transmutation of authentic artifacts of human life into hollow corporate brand divisions.*

Well, it's hard to think of getting something more wrong than that. I wouldn't quote this negativity except for the fact that he put his finger perfectly on what Cincinnati chili is all about, and he said it was the opposite. Cincinnati's signature dish is ingrained in the city's culture and its way of life; it's a dish that makes a deep connection between residents

The Camp Washington Chili sign was saved from the original building when Colerain Avenue was widened, and it now sits on top of the new location across the street. *Courtesy of Carol Highsmith, Library of Congress.*

and their city. Immigrants came up with it in a literal and figurative melting pot, mixing the old and new worlds. It is an authentic artifact of human life. If you have lunch with downtown office workers wearing bibs at the Skyline on the corner of Fourth and Sycamore Streets on any weekday, stop in Pleasant Ridge Chili after midnight or try to get a table at Price Hill Chili before an Elder High School football game, you'll know how close chili is to the Cincinnati heart.

People in Cincinnati eat chili to the tune of two million pounds a year, according to the Greater Cincinnati Convention and Visitor's Bureau. The chili chain Skyline has the highest loyalty of any sit-down chain restaurant in the country, according to a study done by research firm InMarket in 2017. The chain gets returning customers at a rate 27 percent higher than average. In third place is Cincinnati's Frisch's Big Boy, which has an 18 percent higher return rate than usual. Again, Cincinnatians are either commendably loyal or stubbornly stuck in their ways.

There are two large chains that sell Cincinnati chili, but many neighborhood parlors, diners and lunch restaurants that don't have "chili" in their name also sell chili. Consumers can buy it canned and frozen, and they can buy spice packets to try to re-create the "secret" recipe from their favorite chili place. If you go to a few parties in Cincinnati, you'll be able to try the chili layered with sour cream as Skyline dip. It's served at Reds, Bengals and University of Cincinnati games. Cincinnati chili has its own lingo, secret menu, mysteries about its ingredients, controversies, rivalries and myths—it is a folk food.

The original owners of Skyline did sell the chain in the 1990s. Today, it's owned by eight members of management, but the essentials of the Skyline restaurants, like the counters and speedy service, remain the same. The franchise owners in many locations are from original immigrant families and have their own relationships with their communities. Gold Star Chili is still owned by the Jordanian family who started it, and neighborhood chili

Lunch rush begins at Price Hill Chili on Cincinnati's west side in 2012. *Courtesy of the* Cincinnati Enquirer *and Glenn Hartong.*

parlors and cafés are as far from corporate as it's possible to be—most of them are neighborhood spots that have been owned by Greek families for several generations. The Deadspin writer's number-one pick, Chicago pizza, could just as easily be accused of commodification and overuse of cheese. The idea that the city's enthusiasm for Cincinnati chili would have to be artificially pumped up is absurd. "More for us," would be the response of most Cincinnatians to this diatribe; Cincinnatians continue to wear a path from their offices or homes to their favorite chili purveyor.

People complain, "But it's not chili!" I guess that's an understandable grievance. The best way to understand Cincinnati chili's origin is to look at hot dog sauce in New York, but let's start in Macedonia. This is a region in the Balkans that has long been politically contested and ethnically mixed. The region has various languages, religions and ethnicities, from Bulgarian and Turkish to Albanian and Greek. Various powers took over from each other—not always peacefully. It's exactly the kind of situation that has always sent immigrants to the United States; those immigrants went to New York first.

Macedonians and Greeks started coming to the United States in the early twentieth century, and many ended up in the vicinity of Coney Island. Today, when we think of Coney Island, we think of hot dogs, but at the time, there were no hot dogs there officially. There was a fear,

Right: A giant inflated cheese coney mounted on a billboard on I-71 in 1983. *Courtesy of the* Cincinnati Enquirer *and Gordon Morioka.*

Below: Johnny Johnson, the owner of Camp Washington Chili, celebrating the seventy-fifth anniversary of the chili parlor in 2015. Johnson came to Cincinnati from Greece in 1951. *Courtesy of the* Cincinnati Enquirer *and Liz Dufour.*

apparently, that people would think they were actually made of dogs, so they called them "Coney Islands," and they were sold with chili sauce on top. Greek-Macedonian immigrants gravitated to businesses that sold hot dogs because they were cheap and easy to make. When these immigrants struck out from New York to find places to settle, they took their hot dog businesses with them. In Michigan, the Greek-Macedonians called the establishments "Coney Islands" as well. Today, Detroit and other cities in Michigan are crazy for coneys, which come in a variety of formulations. Some are made with a ground beef heart chili (and people think Cincinnati chili is weird).

Three brothers from Macedonia, the Kiradjieffs, moved to Cincinnati and opened one of these Coney Island joints. It was in a good location, just inside the Empress Burlesque Theater downtown, so their establishment was also called Empress. There, the brothers sold Coney Islands, but they spiced the chili sauce with flavors from their homeland, with its crossroads of Slavic, Greek, Albanian and Turkish cooking. Warm spices, like cinnamon, were part of that heritage, and they were mixed into savory foods as well as sweet. Those spices gave their chili sauce a brand-new flavor profile, one that has been beloved and maligned ever since. (Outsiders sometimes seem almost offended by the cinnamon.) They did something else with the sauce: they mixed it with spaghetti. Customers liked it but suggested changes: why not put the sauce on top of the spaghetti, and how about some cheese? Who knows how much cheese they started with—surely not the piles we now get. The basics of Cincinnati chili were set at the Empress.

Cincinnati chili is largely thought of as Greek, even though the originators were more Greek-adjacent. The Kiradjieffs were Slavic, but they were Greek Orthodox. The Greek and Macedonian community in Cincinnati wasn't large enough to keep distinctions. They belonged to a church that served the Greek community. They hired other Greek immigrants who then spread the concept as they opened their own places. It is not the nature of immigrant restaurant owners to mess with a winning formula, and the coneys and spaghetti and cheese prototype was simply reproduced. At some point, the nomenclature of "ways" came into being.

The first chili apostle was Nick Sarakatsannis, who, in 1929, opened Dixie Chili across the river in Kentucky, so as not to compete with the guys who gave him a job. There are still three Dixie Chili locations that are set up to order food at the counter and pay in advance. Though Sarakatsannis duplicated Empress, Dixie Chili has branched off just a little bit by offering a six-way, a five-way with minced garlic on top.

Steve Andon and Fred Zannbus opened Camp Washington Chili in 1940, Peter and Harry Vidas opened Chili Time in St. Bernard in 1943, Samuel and Carl Gerros opened Latonia Chili Parlor in 1946 and Nicholas Lambrinides opened Skyline in 1949. The Sideris family opened Pleasant Ridge Chili in 1964. Chili families are often joined by marriage or employment. In the smallish world of Cincinnati Greeks, with, now, only one Orthodox church, chili is a connecting network.

One important chili family came later and had a different story. The Daouds are from a small Christian village in the mountains of Jordan. Starting in the late 1950s, nine of the ten siblings in the Daoud family immigrated to the United States. Four of them, Basheer, Dave, Charlie and Frank (the names they went by in the United States), came to Cincinnati and tried all kinds of jobs to make it here; they sold old clothes, worked at Spring Grove Cemetery and sold subscriptions to the *Enquirer*. Eventually, the siblings put their money together and bought a lunch spot in Mount Washington called Hamburger Heaven. They paid partly with a loan from the company that installed the jukebox and cigarette machine. The siblings

Lambert Lambrinides (*left*) and Christie Lambrinides (*right*), the sons of the founder of Skyline Chili. *Undated photograph courtesy of the* Cincinnati Enquirer.

made burgers, chili and other luncheonette foods. Dave tinkered with the chili recipe, and it began outselling everything else. So, they renamed their restaurant Gold Star and started the business that turned into one of the two most recognizable and favorite chili chains in Cincinnati. The siblings franchised, designed a prototype store design and put in the first drive-through. For a while, they hired non-family members as CEOs; then in 2015, Roger David, Charlie's son, took the top job.

If you stop in a Skyline, Gold Star or other chili parlor, here's what will happen: your server will come to your table with a dish of oyster crackers and expect that you will order right away. Most people have a standard order and no need for the printed menu. (Though the chains, like Skyline and Gold Star, keep adding non-chili items.) Your chili will arrive soon after—barely long enough for you to carefully bite a small hole in the corner of an oyster cracker and add a few drops of hot sauce to it to eat as an appetizer. (You don't have to do that, but do it once and you always will.) The chili crackers are free and expected. In 2017, Skyline briefly changed its brand of cracker, and the city had a minor conniption fit. Chili places are always speedy, whether you sit at the counter or a table. You'll notice the people forking up spaghetti and ladling on chili because they're always in view, and they are often grown men wearing ties under their aprons. They are probably part of the family of the franchisee who owns the restaurant.

You'll have to decide what "way" you want your chili; you could just get spaghetti and chili, but no one ever really calls that a two-way. Add cheese, and it's a three-way; add beans and onions, and it's a five-way. So, a four-way is a three-way with either beans or onions on it. The onions are chopped and raw and the beans are usually kidney beans, though Dixie uses pinto beans. The server will then ask if you want a bib, and they will tie it on you if you say yes. It's a pretty good idea, because the ends of slurped-up spaghetti have a way of randomly flinging spots of chili onto your blouse or tie. The chili is a lot neater if you eat it the way you're supposed to eat it: cut up. That way, you also maintain the structure of the layers. If you find you especially like the part of the cheese that has melted a bit against the hot chili, next time, you can ask for it to come upside down, with the cheese between the spaghetti and the chili. If you think it's too soupy, ask for it dry, or if you like that aspect, order it juicy.

If you get coneys, they're diminutive three-inch hot dogs in matching buns, topped with chili. The choices here are whether to get a plain coney or a cheese coney, and further decisions can be made about mustard and onions. Or you can consider the hot dog itself optional and get a chili-cheese

A table mid-meal at Camp Washington Chili. *Courtesy of Raúl Arias.*

sandwich instead. Some people wonder if you can just get a plain bowl of chili. Sure, you can. But unlike other kinds of chili, there's not much in the way of texture and taste contrasts in just the chili. But if you're not eating carbs or gluten, you could get a bowl with chili, beans and cheese, I guess. One last thing: you're going to pay at the front counter, where they will have a small box of York Peppermint Patties. You should grab one; it's the final, rounding-off touch.

A funny thing about chili parlors: with well over two hundred chili places in Greater Cincinnati, you would think that the formula for eating and making it would start to diverge, that someone would think it might be a competitive advantage to serve it on, say, ziti, or offer chopped tomatoes or pepperoncini as a garnish, make full-sized hot dog coneys or even serve the chili in a round bowl. But, no, there are only a few ways to serve chili. Dixie Chili offers garlic as a six-way. Blue Ash Chili offers "bottlecaps," or fried jalapenos, for their six-way. They also make chili lasagna. The oyster crackers might be a different brand, and sometimes you can get Andes Mints as well as York Peppermint Patties after eating chili.

The main difference comes in the chili recipe itself, so the different recipes are kept secret—it's part of the shtick. It always has beef, some kind of tomato, cinnamon, cumin and something spicy. People decry the cinnamon, but it comes from an authentic place. I once spent some time with Greek families who prepare vast amounts of pastitsio at Holy Trinity–St. Nicholas Greek Orthodox Church's festival, Panegyri. Their meat sauce is reminiscent of chili in texture and taste. I watched one woman dust every pan with sprinkles of cinnamon. There's a lot more in the recipe, and there have been many recipes published that have claimed to be the authentic one. They include everything from Worcestershire sauce to red wine vinegar, bay leaves, oregano, chicken broth, brown sugar, coriander, celery seeds and sherry. Some recipes say to brown the beef before adding other ingredients. (This is not authentic. Chili parlors just add the beef to liquid. It should be stirred vigorously, breaking up the beef.) Some say to use tomato paste, while others say to use tomato sauce or sometimes even chopped tomatoes. And everyone seems to think that the true secret ingredient is chocolate. Dan Woellert, the history food blogger, is convinced that's a myth. He talked to a lot of chili people for his book, and he said that all of them deny using chocolate. Personally, I'm drawn to the idea that the secret might be sherry.

Cincinnatians' favorite chili is likely to be the one they grew up with or the first one they tried. But there are certainly discernable differences between each chili that could keep a chili head busy for a long time, going from parlor to parlor and chain store to local diner. An interest from television and national press members in regional foods brought outside attention to chili culture, but Cincinnati chili hasn't travelled well or caught the imagination of outsiders. There are national chains that sell Buffalo chicken wings and Philly steak sandwiches, but there is very little Cincinnati chili outside Cincinnati.

Many chili parlors now offer more than just coneys and ways (like three-, four- or five-ways). Skyline has burritos and chilitos, and Gold Star has chili cheese fries and burgers. Smaller parlors have whole menus, chili being just one item. But there's one other dish that historically goes with chili: the double-decker sandwich. These sandwiches are built with three slices of toasted white bread; one ingredient goes between slices one and two, another goes between two and three. The double-decker is not exclusive to chili shops; the club sandwich, for instance, is often served as a double-decker and has been around since around 1900. A Wheel famous toasted double-decker at the Wheel Café was advertised in 1931 for twenty cents, and advertisements for double-decker sandwich makers appeared throughout the 1930s. Another reader told me that, as a girl, she ate double-deckers at her parents' tearoom.

A double-decker sandwich, which can be found in many Cincinnati chili parlors. This one was made with ham and egg salad. *Courtesy of Raúl Arias.*

The sandwiches associated with chili parlors are overstuffed, often with two kinds of meat. There are combos: turkey and bacon or egg salad and ham (my favorite), American cheese, et cetera. The ultimate double-decker sandwich is called a hippo, and it is surely a Cincinnati invention. Hippos are triple-decker sandwiches made with ham, roast beef, cheese or egg and lettuce, tomato and mayonnaise. It's supposed to have the same ratio of height to width that a hippopotamus might. Bob Economou told me his uncle Harry Sarros invented the hippo in 1930 at the Marathon Inn in Silverton. You'll find hippos on various menus. Blue Ash Chili doesn't call their ham and beef sandwich a hippo, but Blue Ash is especially known for its sandwiches—mostly for how large they are. Blue Ash was even featured when Guy Fieri filmed *Diners, Drive-Ins and Dives* in Cincinnati. I'm a fan of the double-deckers at J&J on the West Side.

One more chili parlor menu item that is worth mentioning is the Greek salad. Greek salads were added to the menu at Skyline in 1998 to add a green alternative. I always get one when I have the chili there. The salad has changed over the years, but there's still real Kalamata olives and feta cheese on it. Some other chili parlors, like Price Hill, Dixie and Camp

This photograph was taken for a 1999 story about Maisonette and Skyline Chili celebrating their fiftieth anniversaries in the same month. Jodie Hopcia, a server at Skyline Chili, is holding cheese coneys while Richard Brown, a maître d' at Maisonette, is holding a magnum of Dom Perignon. *Courtesy of the* Cincinnati Enquirer *and Michael E. Keating.*

Washington, also offer this healthier tribute to their ethnic background. My favorite order is a large Greek salad and a couple of coneys with cheese and mustard but no onions.

The same year that Skyline opened—the same month, even—another restaurant opened downtown, and it was completely different; Maisonette's *Mobil Travel Guide* stars were always a point of pride for Cincinnati.

13

THE FIVE-STAR CITY

Fine Dining

In 2013, Boca restaurant opened downtown with a gala celebration. Its young owner and chef, David Falk, had first launched Boca in 2001, taking over a restaurant that was already named Boca in Northside. The restaurant then operated in Oakley for years. Now, the restaurant was opening at its new location at 112 Sixth Street, in the heart of downtown. Many of the glamorously dressed attendees had often walked through the restaurant's red doors in the past, when the balconied building held Maisonette, Cincinnati's famous restaurant that kept five stars from the *Mobil Travel Guide* for forty-one years—longer than any other establishment in North America.

The restaurant the crowd walked into was nothing like the former foyer of Maisonette, where patrons checked their coats, met the maître d' and walked down a few steps into the pink, refined dining room that was filled with fine art and beautifully set tables. Instead, the room featured a floating stairway that hung over the open room, a window that looked into the kitchen and concrete walls that were left bare and patchy in places. The Belle Époque atmosphere meeting bare walls evoked history, nostalgia and luxury. A huge French chandelier was hung in such a way that when you were on the second-floor mezzanine, you were eye-level with its glittering crystals. Ron Novak from the architecture firm Drawing Department said the key word for the project was "disarm."

Yet, if you'd been to Maisonette, you knew it was the same place. It had a side room that was brick-walled and a little less public. And in one corner,

Left: A giant chandelier hangs from the second floor in the middle of the dining room of Boca restaurant downtown in 2013. *Courtesy of the* Cincinnati Enquirer *and Jeff Swinger.*

Below: Boca chef David Falk greets Chef Jean-Robert De Cavel at the door of Boca Restaurant for a twentieth-anniversary party for De Cavel. *Courtesy of the* Cincinnati Enquirer *and David Sorcher.*

a round table was tucked into a niche, with curtains that could close; it looked like it was probably the best table in the city, as a similar one had been for many years. Members of the Comisar family, who were once the owners of Maisonette, were at the party. Jean-Robert de Cavel, who'd been the chef and Falk's boss there, looked at the space with some envy while simultaneously congratulating his protégé.

It was a bittersweet occasion. It was bitter because the closing of Maisonette had been a sad, protracted loss. It closed despite having never lost its five-star rating. And the occasion was sweet because the fine-dining legacy of Cincinnati was being reborn and redefined in a modern way. Boca's owner, Falk, had worked at Maisonette from 1996 to 1998, and it was where he had fallen in love with the kitchen. He had gone to the Culinary Institute of America, much to the bewildered reaction of the private-school world he came from. For him to open a restaurant in that space was an homage to a tradition that was something of a specialty of Cincinnati. Cincinnati has a history of fine dining, and Boca was a legitimate scion of the tradition.

People are very fond of saying that Cincinnati used to have three five-star restaurants at a time when New York had four and San Francisco only had two. While that was true, it was only for a very short period of time in 1970 and 1971. Maisonette had the top rating from 1964 to 2009—an extraordinary run. Pigall's on Fourth Street earned the five stars in 1967, but in the 1972 *Guide*, they were down to four stars; in 1973, they weren't listed at all. Then they gained the stars back in 1975 and 1976. The Gourmet Room, which was on the roof of the Terrace Plaza, was first given five stars in the *Guide* in 1970, but in the 1974 edition, they were down to four. All three restaurants were traditional French restaurants, though they varied a bit. John Kinsella, who came to the Gourmet Room as a chef in 1975, said that Maisonette was haute cuisine, the Gourmet Room was Parisian-style and Pigall's was "provincial."

There's never been an American restaurant guide that carries the seriousness and prestige of France's *Guide Michelin*, but the *Mobil Travel Guide* comes closest. The guide was launched in 1958, when Mobil began sending out anonymous paid staff to review restaurants, hotels and spas. They gave very few five-star ratings (defined as unusually unique and distinctive dining experiences, with exceptional food, superlative service and elegant decor). It's hard to explain why Cincinnati should have had three of them, although there is no doubt that the Fortune 500 companies headquartered in the city, including Procter and Gamble, Federated Department Stores, Kroger and Milacron, were key. In the

1960s and 1970s, the companies' executives had more generous expense accounts than they do today. Some glamorous guests came through town to perform at Beverly Hills Supper Club in Southgate, Kentucky, or on WLW-TV, a national broadcaster. Perhaps it was because of Cincinnati's good downtown department stores, which drew in customers from all over the Midwest, that made it possible to maintain fine dining. Maisonette always relied on out-of-towners, but I think the Cincinnatians who were wealthy enough to eat French food were a loyal sort, proud of their hometown stars. Mobil's conservative definition of fine dining probably aligned with wealthy Cincinnatians' tastes.

Maisonette held an almost mythical position in Cincinnati for a long time. It wasn't just one of several restaurants; it was *the* restaurant. When I first ate there in the late 1980s, and when I reviewed it several times after I joined the *Enquirer* after 1997, it seemed timeless to me; it was the essential restaurant that did things almost as a duty, following rules about service from a time when they were not optional. Most restaurants today seem like "concepts"; Maisonette just was.

The restaurant was founded by Nat Comisar, the son of a Russian immigrant. He opened a restaurant called La Normandie in 1932 on Walnut Street. In 1949, he added Maisonette, which was located in the basement. He was later married to the former Vallie Karrick from Cynthiana, Kentucky. She knew how to get buzz for the new restaurant; she told people they were full when they were not and even sent waiters with full trays past customers to empty rooms. She deserves a great deal of credit for the success of Maisonette, since Nat died the year it opened. Vallie and her son Lee—joined later by Michael J.—continued running the restaurant. In 1951, Vallie went to New York and came back with a new French chef named Maurice Gorodesky; he had just entered the United States two days before, and he'd had a journey that's hard to really understand these days. He had been employed at the Ritz in Paris before the war; then, after the privations of three years as a prisoner of war in a German camp, he went to the Plat d'Argent, the Caribbean and Canada.

The staff of Maisonette were committed to a high level of dining, and the restaurant earned the five stars for the first time in 1965. Vallie wasn't able to enjoy that triumph, however, as she died in 1964. The next year, her son moved both restaurants to Sixth Street, flipping their positions; Maisonette was on top, and La Normandie was in the basement, where there was a big freestanding fireplace. In 1956, Gorodesky reported that he took the job because it appealed to his "missionary spirit" and that he had to work to convert Cincinnatians to this sophisticated cuisine. He said that one local

The corner curtained table at Maisonette—the best table in the city for many years. *Courtesy of the* Cincinnati Enquirer *and Craig Ruttle.*

told him that Cincinnatians would accept change, "but they liked to build up a gradual immunity to it."

Many of the local reactions to Mobil and others' accolades of the restaurant seemed to strike a note of "What? Little old us?" In 1956, the *Enquirer*'s "Talk of the Town" column announced a Holiday award for Maisonette, saying, "Let it be known that our town is on first name terms with crepes Suzette as well as apple strudel and sauerkraut." Dorothea Hake, the food editor at the *Enquirer* in 1953, reported a conversation with Vallie that included the interesting fact that Maisonette served more snails than any other restaurant in the country.

In 1956, Gorodesky left Maisonette to open his own restaurant called Pigall's. The top chef position at Maisonette then went to Pierre Adrian. Like Gorodesky, Adrian had had a rough war experience. He had spent the war forcibly conscripted in the German army and then, after he deserted, joined the French Underground. He had come to Cincinnati in 1951 and worked at Maisonette as an assistant chef. He was head of the Gourmet Room for a few years before going back to head the kitchen at Maisonette, which he did until he died at the age of forty-six in 1972.

The chefs at Maisonette were always French. In 1966, *Mobil Travel Guide* had a gala dinner in New York for all of its five-star chefs. There were eight of them, and they were all men; none of them was born in the United States, and six were either French or Belgian, including Pierre Adrian and Gorodesky.

The Gourmet Room was a last-minute addition to the Terrace Hilton, the absolutely up-to-date modernist hotel and retail building on Sixth Street, between Vine and Race. Today, it is empty and looks like a large blank wall of brick, but it was striking and trendsetting at the time. The hotel opened in 1948 and was developed by John J. Emery, who had developed Carew Tower and the Netherland Plaza. It was designed by Skidmore, Owings & Merrill; a young architect named Natalie de Blois, who was only twenty-four years old, was the lead designer, taking on assignments while her colleagues were in the service. At the last minute, Emery requested a penthouse restaurant on the twentieth floor. The building's design didn't exactly include a penthouse,

The Gourmet Room atop the twentieth floor of the Terrace Hilton Hotel in 1961. The restaurant's Joan Miró mural is visible through the window. *Courtesy of the* Cincinnati Enquirer.

so de Blois added a glass-walled, circular room on the roof and made it a forty-five-seat restaurant with spectacular views. The restaurant had an almost 360-degree view, except for the wall that held a thirty-foot mural by Joan Miró, the Spanish surrealist, which was commissioned for the space. The restaurant also had a whimsical mural with drawings of Cincinnati landmarks by Saul Steinberg and a mobile from Alexander Calder.

The Gourmet Room was modern in every detail and very sophisticated. Clementine Paddleford, the nationally known food writer, visited the hotel in 1952 and got manager Andre Ballestra's recipe for Caesar salad, which was mixed tableside. The restaurant's menu was presented in French and included all kinds of wonderful traditional French dishes. The menu was extensive for such a small restaurant, and it included a salad and cheese course that was listed after the entrées, dessert flambés, game and hot and cold hors d'oeuvres. Beluga caviar, escargots, frog legs amandine, lobster thermidor, veal kidneys flambé, crepes Suzette and peach melba flambé were also on the menu. And everything was made in a tiny, very hot kitchen.

Unfortunately, the Emerys sold the building to Hilton in 1956, and the new owners redid the décor in a French Empire style, with chandeliers and draperies instead of the Miró. But the restaurant won a five-star rating from Mobil in 1970, when there were only twelve restaurants with the distinction in the country. Frenchman Henri Guglielmi was the Gourmet Room's first maître d', and he was the face of the restaurant for two dozen years. He had previously worked in Monte Carlo, where he waited on Winston Churchill and the Prince of Wales. He was described as having a "magnetic personality and subtly flirtatious manner." In his obituary, his daughter said, "He was schooled in Europe, where everything about service is very important."

There was a time when, if you made a reservation at the Gourmet Room, you would find at your table a box of matches embossed with your name. You might order clear turtle soup with sherry, wine-poached sole in cream sauce with mussels and shrimp or braised sliced sweetbreads with paprika and mushrooms and end with sabayon. A lot of the food would be made or flambéed at the table. George Coorey, the restaurant's blind piano player, provided classy background music for thirty-one years. Celebrities, including Lily Pons, Vincent Price, Ella Fitzgerald and President Eisenhower, flitted through the restaurant from time to time.

The Gourmet Room was open until 1992. It sounds like it had gone downhill quite a bit by the end. When Anne Heller, the critic for the *Dayton Daily News*, reviewed it in 1986, she described it as a "pompously decorated restaurant with food that, at times, bordered on a joke." The famous view wasn't the same, as more tall buildings were built downtown. The Terrace Hilton has been vacant for many years, though you can still see the glass room on top of the hotel. It's a hard building to fill, considering that the first seven stories are windowless. The Miró, Steinberg and Calder pieces were given to the Cincinnati Art Museum. (The hotel had painted the Alexander Calder mobile various colors!) The Miró mural is installed just outside of the café at the museum, and the wonderful Steinberg mural, which includes whimsical renderings of Cincinnati landmarks, is in the museum's main entrance hall.

Cincinnati's three five-star restaurants had some close associations, as their employees often moved from one to another. Pigall's (the name is a variation on Pigalle, an area in Paris) was opened in 1957 by Maurice Gorodesky when he left Maisonette. Pigall's was small and charmingly cozy; it served ris de veau a la crème and le caneton roti à l'orange. The restaurant was located on Fourth Street, near Gidding-Jenny, the most upscale women's clothing store in town, and it hosted fashion shows at lunch, a number of ladies' gatherings and meetings, as well as cozy and elegant dinners. Clementine Paddleford visited Gorodesky in 1958, when he told her Cincinnatians loved snails, coq au vin, chicken Nanette and pâté de maison.

Pigall's won its five-star rating in 1967, but in 1972, Gorodesky died of a heart attack. So, in 1973, Mrs. Gorodesky sold Pigall's to Dan Whittle, who had been the maître d' at Maisonette. Because of the change of ownership and the loss of its chef, the restaurant lost its five-star rating that year. Whittle also hired Otis Sherrer, a young African American man from the West End. By 1977, Sherrer was the chef and a subject of a profile in the *Enquirer*. The article detailed a meal that included foie gras d'Alsace, capon Kiev, Dover sole Veronique and quiche Lorraine ("a sort of egg pie with chopped ham and onions"). The restaurant got its five-star rating back in 1978. The restaurant's afterlife was kind of a sad story. It later became Pigall's Café, a nice casual spot with Caesar salads and so on. But when it too folded in 1999, it briefly became a barbecue place called—I don't even like to say it—Pig Al's. Its time was short.

When Pierre Adrian died in 1972, Georges Haidon became the chef at Maisonette. During his tenure, Maisonette continued its tradition, though it relaxed its dress code in the mid-1990s. The classics on the menu were the restaurant's chateaubriand jardinière, a Dover sole, brill en croute, a wonderful café brulot flamed tableside and a dessert cart that always included a white and a dark chocolate mousse. When Haidon retired, the

Comisars wanted to find a new chef who could help them keep Maisonette's five-star rating while making sure the food was up-to-date and keeping pace with all that was new in French cuisine. In keeping with tradition, they hired a Frenchman named Jean-Robert de Cavel, who came recommended by Daniel Boulud in New York. De Cavel was the product of the French system of training and apprenticeship. He was from northern France and began his career with the Rostang family. He then went to New York on a lark but stayed long enough to become chef at La Regence at the Hôtel Plaza Athénée. He moved to Cincinnati to have a five-star restaurant on his résumé, but he didn't know if he'd stay long. As it turns out, he and Cincinnati had a decades-long love affair.

Though Cincinnati had had favorite chefs before, de Cavel's career in the city began in the age of celebrity chefs, foodies and Food Network watchers. He has been a visible presence from the beginning; he is hardworking and voluble, fulfilling everyone's image of the French chef. While the lobster bisque and brill en croute had to remain on the menu, his food at Maisonette was wider-ranging and more contemporary, though it was always carefully composed and used the classic French sauces. In 1996, the restaurant stopped

Nat Comisar, co-owner; Brad Anderson, maître d'; Michael Comisar, co-owner; and Jean-Robert de Cavel, chef de cuisine, celebrating Maisonette's thirty-seventh consecutive Mobil five-star rating in 2001. *Courtesy of the* Cincinnati Enquirer *and Gary Landers.*

describing every dish in French on the menu. De Cavel continued to help earn the stars for the restaurant.

In 2001, I sat down at a table at Maisonette for a review; I unfolded the napkin at my place and found two worn spots on it that were about to turn into holes. I didn't make too big a deal of it, but looking back, it did seem like an omen. By this time, de Cavel had left, though he had been replaced by another very good French chef named Bertrand Bouquin, and the restaurant was struggling—2001 had been a terrible year. There was a Delta Airlines strike, impacting tourism and conventions; then, in April, there were riots in Over-the-Rhine over a police shooting, leaving people somewhat irrationally reluctant to come downtown—then came 9/11. Downtown was poised for a comeback, but it was still pretty dead after office hours. Nat Comisar floated various plans (to add a nightclub, to move to Northern Kentucky or Kenwood), but the money to make any of these plans possible never materialized. He asked the city for money but was turned down.

Finally, and apparently suddenly, Maisonette and La Normandie closed their doors on July 5, 2005. The restaurant's assets were sold at auction—including everything from the fine art to the sauté pans, the wine cellar and the restaurant's name itself. It was a sad day, but the restaurant had held onto its five-star rating until the very end. In a way, it was the end of an era in Cincinnati, but Maisonette lives on in the world of fine dining in the city. Many of the chefs and restaurant owners in Cincinnati were trained in the Maisonette kitchen. The kitchen had always been run on the classic French brigade system, a hierarchical arrangement in which each person in the kitchen had an assigned station, from the garde manger and fish cook to the sous chef. Young cooks, whether they'd cooked elsewhere or had no experience at all, could prove themselves, learn at every station and move up the hierarchy. Having "formerly of Maisonette" on a cook's résumé is like having a personal star.

Jean-Robert de Cavel had left Maisonette to open his own restaurant in 2002. In keeping with tradition, his new place was on Fourth Street, in the old Pigall's space. The building had sat empty after Pig Al's demise, but with financial backing from Martin and Marilyn Wade, he opened a new fine-dining restaurant that was very sophisticated. This was the second phase of his career in Cincinnati. Maître d' Richard Brown, who had a mental rolodex of fine-dining customers in his head, came with him from Maisonette. They put together a skilled team, and de Cavel was prepared to serve the kind of French food that he was good at making in a beautiful, tasteful dining room. While he was working on getting the restaurant open, his newborn daughter died of sudden infant death syndrome. Her death devastated de Cavel and his wife, Annette Pfund de Cavel, but they did open Pigall's. He and Annette created a SIDS foundation that continues to raise money to fight the syndrome to this day. I wrote in my first review:

> *There will be a moment...when everything will stop. When the dishes of each course are set in front of you, conversation will cease, and, just for a moment, you'll simply look and anticipate. You will notice the impossibly tiny melon balls with the crab, enjoy the sheen of a reduced sauce or the jaunty arrangement of wedges of cheese on the cheese plate....The food is always French and always haute, but never stiff. Its artisan touches are local ingredients and seasonal styles.*

Then, with the Wades' money behind him, de Cavel went on to open several other restaurants: a French-Vietnamese restaurant, an informal French bistro and a café, a farm-to-table spot in Covington and a café in an old laundromat that was the first of the restaurants to open on Vine Street in Over-the-Rhine. Then, publicly and bitterly, there was a break between him and the Wades, and Pigall's closed. The other restaurants

Chef Jean-Robert de Cavel (*center*) on the last night of Jean-Robert at Pigall's downtown in 2009. *Courtesy of the* Cincinnati Enquirer *and Jeff Swinger.*

stayed open for varying amounts of time, but they eventually closed their doors as well.

This is when the third phase of de Cavel's career began. He opened Jean-Robert's Table, which served food as lovely as Pigall's but in a less rarefied atmosphere. Bar a Boeuf is more casual, still, with a loosely interpreted bistro menu. Then came French Crust, which was opened across from Findlay Market, where de Cavel's extensive collection of French posters and salt and pepper shakers ended up. Restaurant L brought back the truly fine-dining atmosphere, with Limoges china, heavy linens and fine service that was presided over by Richard Brown. It has never replaced Maisonette in Cincinnati's imagination, and it closed during the coronavirus shut-down of 2020.

Boca continues to dazzle in the old Maisonette, with a combination of French and Italian dining. It offers a number of different experiences, including sitting on stools overlooking the kitchen, in comfortable

David Falk when he was the chef and owner of Boca's first location in Northside in 2002. *Courtesy of the* Cincinnati Enquirer *and Steven Herppich.*

Boca's beet and goat cheese Mezzaluna salad with aged goat cheese, hazelnuts and greens. *Courtesy of the* Cincinnati Enquirer *and Jeff Swinger.*

persimmon-colored leather banquettes or in separate rooms upstairs. The restaurant offers a sleek modern version of a staid classic, beef wellington. The restaurant has also brought back one of Maisonette's beloved turns: pommes soufflé, thin slices of potato cooked twice so they puff into lovely crisp globes. There's also a hamachi crudo on the menu, as well as chicken with risotto.

Orchids is in that same high category. It's the fine-dining restaurant housed in Cincinnati's most beautiful building, the Netherland Plaza Hotel on Fifth Street. Built in 1939 in the style of French art deco, the hotel is an extravaganza of fanciful sculpture, Brazilian rosewood, German silver, ornate details and grand spaces. Doris Day, the former Doris Anne Kappelhoff of Cincinnati, had her first professional engagement in the Pavilion Caprice. There was also an ice-skating rink in the Continental Room. Winston Churchill once stayed in the hotel, along with a parade of other mid-century celebrities. Today, Orchids is in the Palm Court, which was at one time the hotel's lobby. The restaurant particularly thrived with exciting, modern food during the time Todd Kelly was its executive chef and food and beverage director. I once went up to the rooftop with him to get a look at the beehives he kept up there as a source of local honey. In my review from 2017, I said:

> *I used to feel conspicuous sharing plates with my companions when I ate out, passing them around the table or gathering bites from every dish so I could try everything. Now, of course, everyone does this. And takes photos. Do not do this if you dine at Orchids.... The dishes here are beautiful, self-contained artistic creations, and if you try bites from several, you've messed with the proportions and the experience. There is a progression through each prix-fixe dinner, whether three courses or ten. Each dish contains a multitude of flavors, textures, new discoveries and moments of perfection.*

Anyone who's had it remembers the restaurant's lobster salad topped with a poached egg, wrapped in pastry and deep-fried. Orchids remains dedicated to fine dining in the old style, with silver cloches on the dishes raised in unison.

There is one more important fine-dining story in Cincinnati, and it goes nowhere near France. It's the story of the restaurants of Jeff Ruby, and it has no special historical precedent except for the history of eating steak dinners in restaurants. And Ruby, like many of the earliest settlers of Cincinnati, including John Cleves Symmes, came from New Jersey. He told his life story quite frankly in his autobiography, *Not Counting Tomorrow*. He had a difficult childhood and largely raised himself. He ran away from home at the age of sixteen and spent several weeks sleeping under the boardwalk. He sometimes worked in his stepfather's restaurants, played football in high school and was always on the search for father figures. He eventually got himself to Cornell, where he played football and earned a degree in hotel and restaurant management.

Ruby came to Cincinnati as the manager of a Holiday Inn, and he turned the hotel into a bright nightlife center. This was during the era of the Big Red Machine, and there were no bigger celebrities than Pete Rose, Johnny Bench and their teammates in Cincinnati. Ruby made friends with them and with other high rollers in town, and their presence turned his club into a place people wanted to be. He was a genius at running hospitality businesses, though he was also a hothead who'd get in fights.

In 1981, Ruby opened the Precinct in an old police station that was located in an unlikely part of town—it was a huge smash. Everyone went there for both the restaurant and the nightclub bar scene upstairs. Ruby had thought he'd serve French food, but he settled on a steakhouse in the classic mode of the great New York and Chicago steakhouses. However, the restaurant served a lot more than steak. Ruby's second restaurant was located on a barge in the Ohio River, in Covington. The complex was

Left: A menu from Restaurant Continentale at the Netherland Plaza (now called Palm Court), which featured entertainment from ice skaters on an indoor rink. *Courtesy of the Hilton Netherland Plaza.*

Right: The grand space at the Netherland Plaza, which is now the Palm Court, was once the lobby of the hotel. *Courtesy of the* Cincinnati Enquirer.

Jeff Ruby in front of his new restaurant, Jeff Ruby's, just after it opened in 1999. *Courtesy of the* Cincinnati Enquirer *and Gary Landers.*

called the Waterfront, and the restaurant was called South Beach Grill. This restaurant was even more of a scene than the Precinct, with an outdoor bar, a waterfall and a glossy white piano with a pianist. For a while, there was a restaurant upstairs that I remember as one of the best Italian restaurants I've been to in Cincinnati. Carlo and Johnny in the suburbs came later, as did Jeff Ruby Steakhouse downtown.

Ruby was a perfectionist when it came to running his restaurants; he was an avid reader of comment cards and a constant presence at the Precinct. He did things in a big way, with luscious, big aged steaks, a lot of extravagant seafood and, notably, delicious side dishes. His chef, Jimmy Gibson, kept the menus interesting beyond normal steakhouse standards. Ruby always understood that steakhouses couldn't be exclusively male joints; he thought about women customers and knew that women would be the veto vote. People talked about the Freddy salad and the potatoes Anna as much as they did about the bone-in ribeye steak, the Jeff Ruby.

In 1987, Ruby suffered a traumatic brain injury when he stepped out of his ex-wife's moving car. He wasn't expected to recover but was back at work after eight weeks; he was erratic at first but recovered enough to continue his meticulous hands-on management and expansion of the brand. By 2015, Ruby was sharing the daily running of his restaurants with his daughter Britney. His sons Brandon and Dillon were also involved, especially as the company opened Jeff Ruby Steakhouses in Louisville, Columbus, Indianapolis, Nashville and Lexington. He gained some national notoriety when he kicked O.J. Simpson out of his Louisville restaurant in 2007. That strong feeling he had about Simpson was part of a passion he developed around crime victims' rights—something that started to consume him as he pulled back from the daily running of his restaurants.

It often seems that Jeff Ruby wishes he was Italian. He's not, but Cincinnati has an Italian food presence that is not as well-known as its German and Greek counterparts.

14

SACRED HEART, RAVIOLI AND PIZZA

The Cincinnati Italians

The ravioli at the Sacred Heart Church Ravioli Festival are chubby, chewy packets of homemade pasta stuffed with a mixture of veal, spinach and cheese. They're made from scratch and coaxed through a heavily used ravioli shaper by the members of the church and volunteers from the Sons of Italy. The ravioli festival is held twice a year—once in October and once on Palm Sunday. Part of the experience is waiting in line until there's room at a table in the packed community room. As word has gotten around in recent years, the lines are longer, with people coming from all over town who love the historic and authentic nature of this festival.

The ravioli, or meatballs and spaghetti if you prefer, are served on paper plates and ladled with tomato sauce that is also made from scratch. You'll get some soft Italian bread, salad and, if you're lucky, someone might share some red wine with you. People bring pots to be filled with the ravioli to take home, but it's better eaten on the long, shared tables that are often filled with many members of a family who have been going there for years. The volunteers—most of whom are in their retirement years—spend days getting ready for the event, stirring steaming vats of tomato sauce and passing huge trays of ravioli through a window. But teenagers bring patrons trays of food.

Sacred Heart was originally a German congregation. They built the beautiful Gothic church in Camp Washington, the meatpacking part of town. In 1969, when an Italian congregation's downtown church, also called Sacred Heart, was being torn down, the German congregation merged with the Italian congregation. The church still offers mass in

Diners at the Sacred Heart Church Ravioli Festival in 2019. *Courtesy of Raúl Arias.*

Servers deliver dinners of homemade ravioli and spaghetti to patrons of the semi-annual ravioli dinner at Sacred Heart Church in Camp Washington. *Courtesy of Raúl Arias.*

Latin. The Germans are still the predominant ethnic group in Cincinnati, and the Greeks had an outsized effect on the city's food through their chili. Cincinnati has never exactly been a multi-ethnic city, as it failed to attract a lot of immigrants once its economy slowed after the Civil War—but it's not the whole story.

Italians, in particular, have a larger presence in town than many first realize, and since Italians are crazy about food, there's some good Italian food traditions in the city. Italians had a different immigration story from the Germans; they tended to be poorer and came as single men with the intention of returning to Italy. They came in big numbers during the last couple of decades of the nineteenth century, and there was another wave after World War II. Mostly, the Italians settled in cities on the East Coast or larger American cities like Chicago, but many made it as far as Cincinnati. They tended to go into the garment industry as tailors or seamstresses, doing piece work. Many came during the 1960s and were hired by relatives in those industries. Barbering was another popular Italian profession, but some went into restaurants and food businesses.

Buddy LaRosa, the owner of LaRosa's Pizza, in 2019. *Courtesy of the* Cincinnati Enquirer *and Cara Owsley.*

The LaRosas came from Sicily and went into the fruit business, another popular Italian enterprise. Tony LaRosa was a boxer and a truck driver. He and his more genteel wife, Anna, had a little boy named Donald Sebastian. The marriage didn't turn out so well, but their son, who everyone called Buddy, went on to make a big name for himself. His pizza restaurant, which grew into the chain LaRosa's, became one of those Cincinnati hallmarks that natives get nostalgic for and outsiders don't always quite understand. Buddy himself is beloved for his warmth and generosity, his championing of high school sports, boxing and his restaurants.

LaRosa grew up in Over-the-Rhine and in South Fairmont, which was known as Little Italy. The congregation of the church there, St. Anthony's, was almost completely Italian. As the son of divorced parents, Buddy often felt ostracized but not by his relatives; the aunts and grandmother who cooked for him taught him the value of food and feeding people. He took their lead and their recipes when he opened a pizza place on Boudinot Avenue on the West Side. This was in 1954, when pizza was still a foreign food in the United States. LaRosa hustled to get people to try it and come back; he'd even memorize names and orders. "He wanted to connect with customers when they walked in. He was in the pizza shop the first fifteen years morning, noon and night," said his son Mark LaRosa, who is now the president of LaRosa's. "One relationship, one engagement after another. And it connected with those folks in a way that was pretty special." LaRosa connected where it counted, and he donated pizza to a lot of high school sports teams. He created a large and very loyal group of customers. The restaurant grew through franchising that was done on a handshake. Now, there are more than sixty LaRosa's locations, and it controls about a quarter of the pizza market in Cincinnati.

LaRosa's pizza was created when people didn't know what pizza was, so it was the first version that many Cincinnatians ate. Its taste profile has been imprinted on the city, and even people who like more cutting-edge Neapolitan pizza, thick-crusted Detroit-style or more exotic toppings fall back on LaRosa's when they just want pizza. A high percentage of Cincinnatians remember 347-1111, the centralized telephone number for ordering that was repeated frequently in advertisements.

The oldest continuously operating restaurant in Cincinnati that has stayed in the same family is Italian. Scotti's current space on Vine Street in downtown is not its original location, but the Scoleri family first started serving Italian food in Cincinnati in 1912. No one quite knows why the family's founder came to Cincinnati, but he probably needed to leave Philadelphia for some

Buddy LaRosa visits with customers Marilyn Constable and Lucinda Stewart, both of Western Hills, in 2004. *Courtesy of the* Cincinnati Enquirer *and Steven M. Herppich.*

Buddy LaRosa with three of his earliest employees, his aunt Aurora Urbisci; his mother, Mary; and his daughter, Denise, in 1973. *Courtesy of the* Cincinnati Enquirer *and Mark Treitel.*

An order of green fettuccine carbonara at Scotti's in 2018. *Courtesy of the* Cincinnati Enquirer *and Sam Greene.*

good reason. Some people still remember Tenerina DiMarco and Emilia Scoleri, who were known for their stern manner and enforcement of rules. They may have kicked you out if you cut your spaghetti with a knife or if they didn't like your attitude, and they made sure you finished your food. They even kicked out F. Lee Bailey, the famous defense attorney, though no one now knows what his offense was.

The Scoleris' great-nephews and niece now run the place, and they don't admonish anyone for not finishing—the restaurant's servings are huge. But Scotti's is still different from any other Italian restaurant in town. Inside, it's like another world. With no windows, it could be any time of the day—or of the last century. The Chianti bottles with candles illuminate things dimly, the soundtrack plays opera arias and the servers, who are the owners, are no-nonsense. You can still get all kinds of veal cutlet dishes, a really delicious version of green fettucine carbonara made with spinach pasta, saltimbocca, rolled veal and osso buco at the restaurant. It's one of the few places you can get pasta with chicken livers.

Newport, Kentucky, once had so many Italians that one neighborhood was known as "Spaghetti Knob." Some of the community's Italians played a part in Newport's run as a sort of Atlantic City of the Midwest, where casinos, showrooms and strip clubs made it a miniature Sin City. But well before that era, in 1933, the Pompilios opened a restaurant, named for themselves, in a brick building in the part of town known as Mansion Hill. They ran Pompilio's as an affordable restaurant and meeting place for Italians with two rooms: a bar and a small dining area. The restaurant was expanded to add another dining room, and the place was purchased in 1983 by another Italian family, the Mazzeis. Rose, the matriarch of that family, worked in the commissary for years, making ravioli and other old family recipes. It still has an old-fashioned look,

Above: Wanda Ewing, a server at Pompilio's Restaurant in Newport, takes an order in 2013. *Courtesy of the* Cincinnati Enquirer *and Patrick Reddy.*

Left: Pompilio's Restaurant hosts an ItalianFest bocce ball tournament for mayors and city officials. *Courtesy of the* Cincinnati Enquirer *and Chris Mayhew.*

with a tile-floored bar and red-checked tablecloths. It almost looks like the set of a movie. In fact, it was used in the movie *Rain Man* in 1988, though it would have done as well in *The Godfather*. Bocce ball leagues even compete on the court outside. The lasagna is a classic at Pompilio's, and the rigatoni Teresa is layered with a hard-boiled egg, marinara and a meatball. The restaurant also serves braciola, and the ravioli are still named for Rose Mazzei.

The Mazzeis, not the Pompilios, were also a part of a community within the Italian community; they were emigrants from a particular town in Calabria called Fuscaldo. It's always been a poor community, and once some of the men came over to the United States and found work, they encouraged their friends and neighbors to come and sent back for their wives and children. When these immigrants did well in the United States, they'd hire relatives in their tailoring business. They had their own society, the Fuscaldese Society, and they tended to live in Mount Auburn, where they attended the Sacred Heart Church (which was then downtown) and shopped at Findlay Market. Today, the society is gone, but the women's version, La Societa Fuscaldese Femminile, still lives on, though it now welcomes any woman of Italian background. The society gets together to make cookies, including for CincItalia, an Italian festival held on the West Side every June. They sell old-fashioned authentic amaretti biscotti, pizzelles, tordilli and much more. They fill cannoli to order, and for family weddings, they might make thirty to forty different kinds of cookies.

Many of the younger generations of the Fuscaldese families, who spent their youth eating at their relatives' houses, making sausages in basements

and growing herbs and tomatoes, have turned to newer food enterprises. The first generation of Ramundos were successful in the tailoring business, while the next generation has two pizzerias and a sausage brand. The Frommeyer brothers, whose mother is Fuscaldese, opened a pizzeria called Buona Vita. Mark Frommeyer and his wife make fine rustic bread at their bakery called Blue Oven. One variety of their bread, the light ciabatta loaf, is called the Fuscaldese. Tony and Austin Ferrari, who grew up in Cincinnati and moved to San Francisco to open a restaurant and a coffee shop, came home to take over their uncle Fausto's barbershop on Garfield Place. They also opened a coffee and wine shop in Camp Washington called Mom 'n 'ems and have a restaurant in the Contemporary Art Center named for Fausto.

Right: Tordelli, one of the many cookies made by La Societa Fuscaldese Femminile to sell at an Italian festival, in 2012. *Courtesy of the* Cincinnati Enquirer *and Joseph Fuqua II.*

Below: The second annual meeting of the Societa Fuscaldese in Gutzwiller's Grove in 1932. *Courtesy of Societa Fuscaldese Femminile.*

Sotto is known for, among other things, its varieties of bruschetta, like goat cheese and hazelnut honey and peperonata with hard-boiled egg and anchovies. *Courtesy of the* Cincinnati Enquirer *and David Sorcher.*

The city's more recent Italian immigrants include Nicola Pietoso and his son Cristian, who came here from Florence. Nicola came first, and he opened Nicola's, a lovely upscale restaurant on the northern edge of Over-the-Rhine; the restaurant was opened long before that neighborhood became an obvious locale for an upscale restaurant, but it has thrived there since 1996. Cristian worked for him before he opened his own contemporary Italian restaurant called Via Vite on Fountain Square. Then he opened two more called Forno, which were built around brick ovens with rustic Italian cooking. David Falk, who's not Italian at all but, as so many chefs do, fell in love with Italy and its cuisine, opened an Italian restaurant in the basement under Boca and called it Sotto. It serves classic Italian and is often mentioned as the best Italian restaurant in town.

15

MADE IN CINCINNATI

Kroger Brand Products

Starting with its earliest enterprises, Cincinnati has made things that other people have wanted. From steamboats and carriages to Baldwin pianos, from Brunswick bars to machine tools, the city's manufacturers have created brand-name products. This is true for the city's food, too. The following are some of Cincinnati's most popular national products, from the 1860s to the modern day.

Crisco

Procter and Gamble, the giant consumer products company headquartered in Cincinnati, began as a soap and candle maker, using animal fats from the Cincinnati meatpacking industry. The company branched out from there, with each new product springing from something it had already made. In 1911, the company introduced hydrogenated cottonseed oil as Crisco shortening (originally called Krispo), which replaced lard. Procter and Gamble introduced Crisco to the country with the largest, most carefully planned advertisement campaign ever used at the time (including copy written by female copywriter Helen Lansdowne Resor). It's been a staple on American shelves ever since. Later, the company developed a zero-trans-fat version, and now, all Crisco is

Crisco and Jif, two iconic Procter and Gamble food products, though P&G sold both of the brands in 2001. *Courtesy of the* Cincinnati Enquirer *and Glenn Hartong.*

made without trans fats. Procter and Gamble made Crisco in Ivorydale, along the Mill Creek, for many years. Crisco was sold to the J.M. Smucker Company in 1992.

KROGER BRAND PRODUCT

Barney Kroger established his shop in 1883 on Pearl Street. His company was a grocery innovator. One thing the company did first was have its own bakery and butcher; that way, shoppers could get everything done in one trip. Kroger continued bringing manufacturing in house until it was the largest food manufacturer in the country—a title it retains today. The company makes its own ice cream, soft drinks, peanut butter and cookies. Much of its manufacturing is still done in Cincinnati.

Two Kroger employees taste coffee in 1958. Kroger has always had many of its own brands, including coffee. *Courtesy of the* Cincinnati Enquirer.

Square Matzos

In 1886, Rabbi Dov Manischewitz emigrated from Lithuania to Cincinnati's West End, which was then a melting pot neighborhood that included Jewish immigrants from all over Europe. He began making matzos for Passover. To be kosher for Passover, matzo making had to be overseen by a rabbi who knew the kosher rules. They had to be baked within eighteen minutes of mixing, and they were always rolled by hand into a circle. Eager to build his matzos into a business, Manischewitz developed a mechanized matzo baking process that created square matzos in 1888. This was controversial; it wasn't just the shape but whether they could still be considered kosher. He used his own reputation to assure customers that they were made with kosher procedures. Jonathan Sarna, a scholar of American Jewish life, said, "[Manischewitz], working within the confines of the Jewish law, managed to synthesize the requirements of the Jewish faith with the most modern of contemporary technologies to produce more matzo for more people than any company in Jewish history." The Manischewitz company moved to New Jersey in 1932, and the Cincinnati plant closed in 1958.

Frank's Hot Sauce

Another Jewish Cincinnati entrepreneur was responsible for the introduction of the hot sauce that made the original Buffalo wings spicy. In 1896, Jacob Frank left a job selling liquor for his father and, along with brother Emil, founded the Frank Tea and Spice Co., which sold spices in small packets. The company was known for treating its employees well, and it introduced

A photo of Frank's Quality Food Products from the book *Frankly Speaking: Fifty Years of Progress. Courtesy of the* Cincinnati Enquirer *and Amanda Davidson.*

profit-sharing, health benefits and pensions. In 1920, the company introduced Frank's Hot Sauce, which was made in Louisiana from vinegar, garlic, cayenne and spices. In 1964, Teressa Bellissimo of the Anchor Bar in Buffalo, New York, used her bottle of Frank's to spice up some chicken wings, and the rest is history. Frank's Hot Sauce was sold to Durkee in 1977 and then to McCormick Spice Co. in 2017. It's common to find Frank's on tables in Cincinnati chili parlors.

McDonald's Filet-o-Fish

Cincinnati's West Side is strongly Catholic, which was obvious to franchise owner Lou Groen on Fridays during Lent, when his business took a dive. He suggested a fish sandwich to McDonald's corporate headquarters in 1962. It went up against another candidate for a meatless alternative: a pineapple sandwich. The fish won that matchup in modified form; the steamed bun with a square piece of fish and a slice of melty cheese has been on the menu ever since.

Pringles

In the 1950s, Procter and Gamble's involvement with cooking fats led the company to think about developing a potato chip. To fit into its distribution networks, the chips had to be sturdily packaged and have a long shelf life. In 1968, they began test marketing Pringles, which were shaped in a fancy

Several varieties of Pringles, the potato snack invented by Procter and Gamble. *Courtesy of Pat Wellenbach and AP Photo.*

saddle-like curve and packed in a tube. But by 1975, sales were declining. The company almost gave up the brand, but it instead starting marketing it to kids, introducing a number of novelty flavors and making the crisps taste better by spraying them with oil. By the late 1990s, it was one of Procter and Gamble's most popular brands. The brand was sold to Kellogg in 2012.

Candy Corn

The familiar orange, yellow and white nuggets that have a polarizing effect every Halloween weren't exactly invented in Cincinnati, but the Goelitz Company first commercially produced them here in 1898. Workers poured the three different-colored liquid layers of buttercream candy into cornstarch-dusted molds in an all-German-speaking workshop. In 2001, the Goelitz Company, which had moved to California, became the Jelly Belly Company.

Fleischmann's Yeast

Charles and Maximilian Fleischmann, Jewish brothers from Hungary, came to Cincinnati from Vienna in the 1860s. They found a big difference in the quality of yeast between Europe and America. Bread in America was made with home-brewed sourdough starters. In 1868, with financial backing from Cincinnati businessman James Gaff, they developed a compressed yeast cake that was reliable, powerful and easy to distribute. They took it to the Philadelphia Exposition of 1876, setting up the "Model Vienna Bakery" as their display. Vienna bread, a light, sweet-fermented white bread, became a huge favorite. In the 1920s, the Fleischmanns went on to manufacture vinegar, margarine and gin. They became extraordinarily rich. During Prohibition, they advertised their yeast as a health cure for things like constipation and acne, creating a fad for eating yeast cakes. During World War II, they developed a dry granulated yeast that did not require refrigeration. Though they eventually moved their business to New York, they remained active in Cincinnati. Charles's son Julius was elected mayor when he was twenty-eight as a reform candidate. He started by reforming the police department. Julius was known nationally as a bon vivant, polo-playing, three-times-divorced millionaire. He is buried in Spring Grove Cemetery in the family's Greek Revival mausoleum.

LITTLE KINGS

The little seven-ounce, green-bottled cream ale was the only beer from Cincinnati that really gained a national presence after Prohibition. At its most popular, Little Kings was distributed to forty-four states. It owes its birth in 1958 to a failed compressor in the beer draft system at the Montgomery Inn, Cincinnati's beloved ribs restaurant. When drafts weren't available, the boiler-maker drinkers didn't want a full-size bottle, so owner Ted Gregory asked Ed Schoenling to give him a smaller bottle of beer. Schoenling chose his cream ale, with its slightly sweet flavor, to go with bourbon. It became a big favorite around Cincinnati and the Midwest. It has always had a special emotional connection for Cincinnatians. Schoenling (a post-Prohibition brewery) merged with Hudepohl (the only surviving pre-Prohibition brewery) in 1986 and continued to make Little Kings, but production left the city in 2001. In 2008, the new Christian Moerlein Brewery, headed by Greg Hardman, began making Little Kings in Cincinnati again.

KAHN'S HOT DOGS

"The wiener the world awaited," a pork hot dog, was made by the Kahn family, who were Jewish. A pork-processing Jewish family wasn't such an anomaly in Cincinnati, where the Reform movement in Judaism first took hold in the United States. The Reform movement emphasized Jewish

The Kahn's inflatable pig floats through the streets during the Findlay Market Opening Day Parade in 2013. *Courtesy of the* Cincinnati Enquirer *and Amanda Davidson.*

principles and downplayed strict kosher laws. Kahn's was opened in 1883 as a meat market, and by 1926, it was one of the largest meatpacking businesses in the country. It was sold to Sara Lee in 1976.

That Strawberry-Flavored Treat or Nacho-Flavored Snack

The industrial flavorings industry got started here as an outgrowth of the whisky rectifying business, which was big in Cincinnati in the nineteenth century. Merchants bought raw distilled liquor from local producers and "rectified" it with flavorings to improve its quality or at least its drinkability. Now, several flavor companies, including Givaudan and Wild Flavors, make flavorings on contract for big food businesses all over the world. Visitors passing by on I-75 can guess by smell what they're making that day.

All of these products bring a little of the history of Cincinnati to eaters across America. They tell the story, if people only knew, of a city that still maintains its roots, that grew from the early Republic, changing with immigration, to finally turn into a typical Midwestern city. But there will always be history to distinguish Cincinnati, and there will always be something else from the city's history that people will draw inspiration from.

ABOUT THE AUTHOR

Photograph courtesy of Meg Vogel.

Polly Campbell grew up in Bloomington, Indiana, and moved to the Queen City in 1983. She immediately got to know the city by shopping for butter bit rolls at the Virginia Bakery; she also shopped for goetta at a now-closed butcher and ate at the Clifton Skyline and Graeter's. In 1996, she became the food writer at the *Cincinnati Enquirer* and began reviewing a restaurant almost every week for twenty years or so. She likes a four-way bean or a Greek salad and two cheese coneys, and she recommends Graeter's toffee chip or a scoop of caramel with bittersweet sauce.